pd 3/7/08

Word Power

Word Power

a guide to creative writing

Julian Birkett

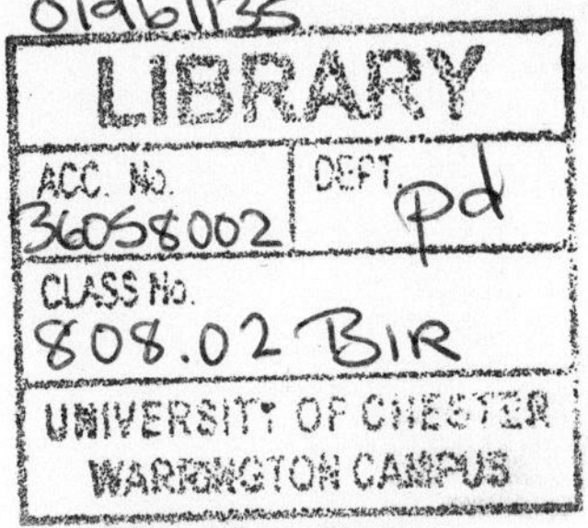
01961135
LIBRARY
ACC. No. 36058002
DEPT. pd
CLASS No. 808.02 BIR
UNIVERSITY OF CHESTER
WARRINGTON CAMPUS

Third edition

A & C Black • London

Third edition 1998
First edition 1983
Second edition 1993
A & C Black (Publishers) Limited
35 Bedford Row, London WC1R 4JH

ISBN 0-7136-4850-3

© 1998, 1983, 1993 Julian Birkett

A CIP catalogue record for this book is available from the British Library.

All rights reserved. No part of this publication may be reproduced in any form or by any means - graphic, electronic or mechanical, including photocopying, recording, taping or information storage and retrieval systems - without the prior permission in writing of the publishers.

Printed and bound in Great Britain by Creative Print and Design (Wales), Ebbw Vale

Contents

Acknowledgements

The following have kindly granted permission for the reprinting of copyright material.

Richard Aldington **Evening**
© The Estate of Richard Aldington. By permission of Rosica Colin Ltd.

Ron Barnes **Willy the Watchmaker**
From *Hackney Writers' Workshop*, Vol. 1. By permission of Centerprise Trust Ltd.

Saul Bellow **The Victim**
Published by Weidenfeld & Nicolson Ltd.

Emily Bishop **Embroidery**
From *Working Lives*. By permission of Centerprise Trust Ltd.

Jorge Luis Borges **The Disinterested Killer Bill Harrigan** and **Notes from Underground**
'The Disinterested Killer Bill Harrigan' from *A Universal History of Infamy* published by Penguin Books 1975, pp. 63–65, Copyright © Emecé Editores S. A. and Norman Thomas di Giovanni, 1970, 1971, 1972; 'Notes from Underground' translated by Jessie Coulson published by Penguin Classics 1972, Copyright © Jessie Coulson,1972; for adaption from *Do You Love Me?* by R.D. Laing published by Penguin Books 1977, p. 25, Copyright © R.D. Laing

Jorge Luis Borges **The Circular Ruins**
From *Labyrinths and Other Stories*. Permission by Laurence Pollinger Ltd. on behalf of New Directions Publishing Corporation. Published by Penguin Books Ltd.

Sandy Brownjohn **Catalogue**
From *Does it Have to Rhyme* published by Hodder and Stoughton Ltd.

Anthony Burgess **A Clockwork Orange**
David Campton **Out of the Flying Pan**
© 1961 David Campton. By permission of Actac Ltd.

Raymond Carver. **Boxes**
First appeared in the *New Yorker Magazine*. First published in Great Britain by Collins Harvill 1988. © Raymond Carver 1986, 1987, 1988. Reproduced by permission of the Harvill Press

Apsley Cherry-Garrard **The Worst Journey in the World**
By permission of Mrs Angela Mathias

Tony Connor **October in Clowes Park**
From *With Love Somehow* published by Oxford University Press

Hilda Doolittle **Oread**
From *Selected Poems of H.D.* By permission of Carcarnet Press

Bob Dylan **A Hard Rain's A-Gonna Fall**
Words and music by Bob Dylan. Copyright © 1963 by Warner Bros. Inc., renewed 1991 by Special Rider Music. All Rights Reserved. International Copyright secured

The Evening Standard
The Evening Standard and Solo Syndication Ltd. for 'Philip Looks in on Solo's Big Clean-Up'

Everyman's Encyclopaedia
J. M. Dent for extracts on Allan Pickerton and Bernard Palissy from *Everyman's Encyclopaedia*, Vol. 6

E.M. Forster **Howard's End**
By permission of King's College, Cambridge and The Society of Authors as the literary representatives of the E.M. Forster Estate,. Published by Edward Arnold (Publishers) Ltd.

Ernest Hemingway **Hills Like White Elephants** and **Soldiers Home**
By permission of Jonathan Cape Ltd. and the Executors of the Ernest Hemingway Estate for 'Hills Like White Elephants' and 'Soldiers Home' from *The First Forty-Nine Stories* and in Canada, Charles Scribner's Sons for 'Hills Like White Elephants' from *The Short Stories of Ernest Hemingway*, © Copyright 1927 Charles Scribner's Sons, © renewed 1955 Ernest Hemingway; and also for 'Soldier's Home' from *In Our Time*, © Copyright renewed 1953 Ernest Hemingway

James Joyce **Dubliners** and **A Portrait of the Artist as a Young Man**
By permission of Jonathan Cape Ltd. and the Executors of the James Joyce Estate

James Joyce **Finnegan's Wake**
By permission of The Society of Authors representing the Estate of James Joyce

Franz Kafka **The Wish to be a Red Indian**, **Passers-By** and **Metamorphosis**
'The Wish to be a Red Indian' and 'Passers-By' from *In the Penal Settlement*, and 'Metamorphosis' from *Metamorphosis* translated by Willa and Edwin Muir, reprinted by permission of Martin Secker and Warburg Ltd.

Barrie Keefe **Sus**
Reprinted by permission of Methuen, London

Philip Larkin **Annus Mirabilis**
From *High Windows*, published by Faber and Faber Ltd.

D.H. Lawrence **The Mosquito Knows**
From *The Complete Poems* of D.H. Lawrence, published by William Heinemann Ltd. By permission of Laurence Pollinger Ltd. and the Estate of Frieda Lawrence Ravagli

Ian McEwan **In Between the Sheets** and **Psychopolis**
From *In Between the Sheets*

Roger McGough **40-Love**
From *After the Merry-making*, published by Jonathan Cape.
Reprinted by permission of the Peters Fraser & Dunlop Group Ltd. on behalf of Roger McGough

Adrian Mitchell **I Like That Stuff**
© Adrian Mitchell. Available in *Blue Coffee: Poems 1985-1996* (Bloodaxe Books, 1996).
Reprinted by permission of The Peters Fraser & Dunlop Group Ltd. on behalf of Adrian Mitchell.
Educational Health Warning! Adrian Mitchell asks that none of his poems are used in connection with any examinations whatsoever

Edwin Morgan **Message Clear**
From *The Second Life*, published by Edinburgh University Press. By permission of Polygon

Bill Naughton **Spiv in Love**
From *Late Night in Watling Street*. Published by Harper Collins. By permission of the Peters Fraser & Dunlop Group Ltd. on behalf of Bill Naughton

Harold Pinter **The Caretaker**
Published by Faber and Faber Ltd.

Peter Porter **A Consumer's Report**
© Oxford University Press 1970 reprinted from *The Last of England* (1970; also in Peter Porter's *Collected Poems*, 1983) by permission of Oxford University Press

Ezra Pound **In a Station of the Metro, Fan-Piece for her Imperial Lord** and **The Encounter**
from *Collected Shorter Poems* by Ezra Pound, published by Faber and Faber Ltd.

Salman Rushdie **Midnight's Children**
Published by Jonathan Cape Ltd.

Sue Shrapnel **Terrace**
From Hackney Writers' Workshop, Vol. 3 by permission of Centerprise Trust Ltd.

Alan Sillitoe **Saturday Night and Sunday Morning**
© Alan Sillitoe 1958, 1986, published by W. H. Allen. By permission of Rosica Colin Ltd.

Les Skeates **By Omission**
From Hackney Writers' Workshop, Vol. 3 by permission of Centerprise Trust Ltd.

Tom Wolfe **The Bonfire of the Vanities**
Published by Jonathan Cape Ltd.

W.B. Yeats **Under Ben-Bulben**
From *The Collected Poems of WB Yeats*. Printed by permission of A.P. Watt Ltd. on behalf of Michael Yeats

The author also wishes to acknowledge with thanks the help of the following:

David Elliot, Judith Graham, Judith Holden, Saleem Peeradina, Chris Taylor, and the following, whose work appears in this book:

Sarah Gillam, Kamal, Darrol Kenworthy, Deepak Manchanda, Dipti Mehta, Fareeda Mehta, Pheruzi, Dipti Shah, Salil Tripathi.

Every effort has been made to trace and acknowledge copyright owners. If any right has been omitted, the publishers offer their apologies and will rectify this in subsequent editions, following notification.

How to use this book

This book is designed to help you learn about imaginative, or creative writing. You cannot be taught how to write, but you can learn about it, as every writer however great or famous has had to learn about it – through writing, through criticism of their writing, through reading, through watching and thinking. The teaching of creative writing in schools, the development of writers' groups, evening classes and community publishers has given an enormous number of people the encouragement to write for their own pleasure and stimulation. The notion of a writer as somebody unique, with a special education and a private income is no longer valid – if it ever was. All that is needed is a willingness to experiment, to develop critical powers, to read what other people have written – and to write.

Don't worry for the moment about publication and fame. The number of people who make a living from their imaginative writing has always been tiny, and big publishers generally take on only a small amount of new fiction. There are a number of different ways in which you can make your writing available other than by having it commercially published. It could mean publication by a community press, a local bookshop or one of what are called the 'little presses'. Or it could mean your reproducing a small number of copies with one of the many reprographic methods now available, such as photocopying, duplicating, or printing on a small offset litho machine.

This book is a practical guide to developing different imaginative writing skills. It covers the established forms of fiction and poetry and the questions which frequently occur when considering them – what kinds of things you should feel confident in writing about, what makes good dialogue, the use of settings, who should tell the story, how to start writing poems or drama, and so on. But it also emphasises the possibilities offered by writing of an experimental nature, looking here at both unpublished and published work. Unusual kinds of short story, poem or drama are discussed, as well as some pieces which don't fit easily into any of these categories. The emphasis throughout is on the small scale, that which is manageable in a limited period of time, rather than on the demands of writing, say, full-length novels.

The final synthesis, the putting together of the different elements discussed in the course of the book, in a poem or story or play, is up to you. No guide can teach you that – you learn about it by doing it. What this book offers you is a wide range of different ways in to imaginative writing, which is why nearly all chapters are followed by a substantial list of ideas for writing. It isn't essential to read the chapters in order, as they do stand on their own, but reference is sometimes made to previous chapters.

The first section of the book concentrates mostly on prose writing, a medium which comes more naturally to many people than poetry, though many of the ideas are also applicable to poetry.

'***Where to start***' suggests that it is useful to bear a couple of things in mind. One is that good writing is generally concrete rather than abstract, is about situations rather than theories. The other is that your own experience is certainly wide enough for you to be able to write interestingly – no need to wander off what you know.

'***Finding a voice***' is about writing monologues, in which you create a character who interests you and who talks for a few pages, and becomes familiar to the reader. It's entertaining to do, and you don't have to worry too much about style or plot – the narrator's personality takes care of most of that.

'***Time to talk***' looks at dialogue, and tries to sort out what it is that makes some dialogue both convincing and interesting and some unbelievable and dull. It also looks at how dialogue and description can enhance each other.

'***Writing about people***' continues this exploration. There are ways of making a character interesting and alive other than straightforwardly describing him or her. The question is, what is the character's function and role in the story?

'***Doing things with places***': the same question applies to places in fiction. Are they designed to provide atmosphere, tell us about somebody, suggest a whole way of life, stand for something in a symbolic way? All these possibilities and more are looked at, with examples.

'***Who's telling the story?***' is an analysis of narrative techniques – first person (the 'I' mode), third person (the 'he/she' mode), and the third person where the focus is on one character. There are advantages and disadvantages with each one, and examples are given.

'***Who's telling the story? – second time around***' looks at a student's short story in the making, from the first to the final draft, and the thinking in between. The story itself tinkers with the question of who is telling the story.

'***The world from the inside***' contains examples of very private, experimental pieces which try to get over the feeling of the individual's inner world.

'***A proper story***' takes a comprehensive look at different kinds of complete short story (those with 'a beginning, a middle and an end')and how you might try writing some of your own. It also includes a reading list of 19th and 20th century short story writers.

The next four sections look at poetry, what it is and how to go about writing it, concentrating again on the small-scale and manageable.

'***What is a poem?***' tries to give a constructive answer to exactly that question, the intention being to make writing poems (and reading other people's) less daunting and more appealing.

'***Just a few lines***' continues along this path, suggesting ways of writing short poems which should give some satisfaction and strengthen confidence.

'***Ideas into shape***' looks at how your ideas can be arranged or 'structured' in a poem in such a way that the poem will take on a clearer shape or 'personality'.

'***New worlds, new forms***' includes examples of experimental writing (and suggestions for your own) which respond directly to the developments of the modern world – computer poems, futuristic language, consumer's reports, civil defence 'manuals', and so on.

Finally '***A bit of drama***': less a guide to how to write conventional plays than a survey of the kinds of situations which make good drama, whether of five minutes' or two hours' duration, and of some different kinds of dialogue.

1 *Where to start*

This opening chapter is concerned with making two broad assertions about imaginative writing. The first is that good imaginative writing is *rooted in the particular*, in particular things, particular people, particular situations, rather than in generalised notions about them. The second, related to this, is that interesting imaginative writing can, and indeed should be, written entirely *from what you know*. Just what it is that you 'know', of course, is a slippery question. What you *don't* know is perhaps easier to judge. While these two assertions are intended to act in some ways as a check, on earnest philosophising on one hand, and on ignorant imitation on the other, they can also be seen as reminders of the possibilities and strengths of imaginative writing.

Rooted in the particular

It really doesn't matter if you want to write but feel you have nothing to 'say' – that is, you don't have a set of opinions or beliefs that you think the world should listen to. In fact this will be a positive advantage. Good writers generally care much more about people, how and why they act and think and feel and speak, and – just as important – about words and what they can do, than about expressing ideas.

The American short story writer, Flannery O'Connor, warned would-be writers against writing not a real story or a poem, but 'a sketch with an essay woven through it, or an essay with a sketch woven through it, or an editorial with a character in it, or a case history with a moral, or some other mongrel thing'.

The writer who ambitiously embarks upon, let us say, a novel specifically about the need for society to accept homosexuality, or the spiritually suffocating effects of mass technology on the individual, runs the risk of producing no more than a sermon on his chosen topic, rather than a novel. His characters are less likely to be believable individuals than pasteboard cutouts designed to illustrate particular social attitudes. For example: A is a homosexual. He is sensitive and good. X is the man who hates A because he releases suppressed homosexual desires in him. Y is the girl who hates A because she finds him threatening to her own female sexuality. Z is the man who understands A and is sympathetic towards him. They are in fact Male Machismo, Female Jealousy and Human Understanding respectively (the last no doubt the author in thin disguise). The novel will have a 'dead' feel to it that a reader won't tolerate. A reader needs to see people and feel sensations in a piece of writing, not be presented with ideas dressed up as something else. The ideas can emerge from the situations, not the other way round.

Many writers describe the germs of things they have written as specific scenes or situations, rather than anything they wanted to tell the world. Harold Pinter's great play *The Caretaker*, about three men who share a dingy room, ceaselessly struggling for dominance within it, is a modern classic. It is constantly performed and constantly reinterpreted, as anything from bleak absurdism to religious allegory. But Pinter has said that the idea for the play came not from a grand idea about humanity, but an image, a glance through a doorway. He was living in a run-down flat in West London, where he used to pass a tramp on the stairs who was evidently staying for a while in the room upstairs with the landlord's brother, a handyman. Then one day he saw them in the room together: 'The image that stayed with me for a long time was of the open door to this room with the two men standing in different parts of the room doing different things . . . the tramp rooting around in a bag and the other man looking out of the window and simply not speaking . . . A kind of moment frozen in time that left a very strong impression.' In that moment Pinter sensed the dramatic potential for a play about relationships and power. Elsewhere he describes how he will often start with a line of dialogue that attracts him, without any idea of where it will take him.

The American short story writer Raymond Carver describes how he wrote a particular story. 'For several days I'd been going around with this sentence in my head: "He was running the vacuum cleaner when the telephone ran." I knew a story was there and that it wanted telling . . . I sat down in the morning and wrote the first sentence, and other sentences promptly began to attach themselves. I made the story just as I'd make a poem: one line and then the next, and the next. Pretty soon I could see a story, and knew it was my story, the one I'd been wanting to write.'

Now Carver and Pinter are very particular kinds of writer, and of course this isn't the way that every writer starts. But most writers would recognise that process, of being intrigued by an image or a phrase or sentence, and trusting their instinct that this was worth pursuing and developing. The point isn't that 'He was running the vacuum cleaner when the telephone rang' is such a brilliant sentence, nor even a brilliant opening. It is that Carver felt he could go somewhere with it. Many other writers wouldn't – but something else might fire them.

Creative writing, unlike journalism or sociology or essay writing, is rooted in the senses. It begins with the concrete. The reason isn't hard to see. After all, we experience our daily lives through our senses, and through our emotions. Creative writing attempts to recapture that vitality, the feel of life as it is lived, not how it is thought about when held at arm's length. How it does this, and to what end, is of course the business of the individual writer. We return to a favourite poem or story with enjoyment, because even if the emotions it produces are sad, what we read is in some way alive. What we respond to, with our senses as well as our minds, is a dramatic reconstruction of reality rather than an essay about it.

What this means in practice (and how it can be done with material always close at hand) may become clearer after looking at the two extracts which follow. Both poems look at the common emotion of affection for familiar objects. One is early 20th century, the other is contemporary. As a result, the tone of voice, the use of language, the choice of objects, is very different. Neither poet speaks in generalities about the things he loves, but confines himself to listing the objects themselves. Nevertheless, we are aware at the end of two wholly different ways of looking at the world.

The first is Rupert Brooke, writing at the turn of the century.

These I have loved:
White plates and cups, clean-gleaming,
Ring'd with blue lines; and feathery, faery dust;
Wet roofs, beneath the lamp-light; the strong crust
Of friendly bread; and many-tasting food;
Rainbows; and the blue bitter smoke of wood;
And radiant raindrops couching in cool flowers;
And flowers themselves, that sway through sunny hours,
Dreaming of moths that drink them under the moon;

Then, the cool kindliness of sheets, that soon
Smooth away trouble; and the rough male kiss
Of blankets; grainy wood; live hair that is
Shining and free; blue-massing clouds; the keen
Unpassioned beauty of a great machine;
The benison of hot water; furs to touch;
The good smell of old clothes; and others such –
The comfortable smell of friendly fingers,
Hair's fragrance, and the musty reek that lingers
About dead leaves and last year's ferns

from *The Great Lover*

Perhaps you can't stand 'white plates and cups . . . ring'd with blue lines'. Tastes change. But there will always be something fresh and vigorous about 'the rough male kiss of blankets'. The comparison gives us an impression of sharply felt, first-hand experience. This is there, too, in the more conventional 'cool kindliness of sheets, that soon smooth away trouble'. There is emotion in the poem, in words like 'friendly', 'kindliness', 'benison', 'comfortable', but what *convinces* us of the friendliness of the bread is its strong crust; we are helped to *feel* the kindliness of the sheets because they are cool. The emotion of the poem reaches us most powerfully at the level of our senses, so that we aren't merely told about these qualities, we feel them in the images (the 'word-pictures') of the poem.

Turning to the language of the poem, though, we immediately run up against a complication. Look at these lines:

And radiant raindrops couching in cool flowers;
And flowers themselves, that sway through sunny hours
Dreaming of moths that drink them under the moon;

Isn't this a bit much, a bit self-consciously 'poetic'? It's dreamy and moony and about flowers so it *looks* like poetry. But do we look at things with a fresh eye after reading this, in the way that we might do after reading 'the rough male kiss of blankets?' No. Because we've heard this kind of thing before. It sounds pretty, but it's second-hand. The tearful lover with pearls on her pillow and all that, pretty-pretty but just not real. For images to work successfully, the language needs to be fresh, so that it seems we are looking at something for the first time.

Here is another, very different, poem about loved objects;

> Lovers lie around in it,
> Broken glass is found in it.
> Grass.
> I like that stuff.
>
> Tuna fish get trapped in it.
> Legs come wrapped in it.
> Nylon.
> I like that stuff.
>
> Eskimos and tramps chew it.
> Madame Tussaud gave status to it.
> Wax.
> I like that stuff.

from 'I Like That Stuff' by Adrian Mitchell

Clearly somebody very different from Rupert Brooke is talking. There is nothing dreamy about Mitchell's poem – by comparison, Brooke appears as a very conventional, romantic young poet. Brooke chooses objects conventionally accepted as beautiful, delicate . . . the mood is one of tenderness, submission, at times almost swooning. His poem even hints at a need on his part for love and reassurance. Mitchell's couldn't be more different. Deliberately choosing materials of an 'unpoetic' or homely nature, he offers a lively appraisal of their varied functions. He takes delight in raking up the most disparate forms or uses his 'stuff' can be put to, and pairing them together – fish and women's legs, eskimos and Madame Tussaud's. Don't we mentally go 'ouch' at the lines:

> Lovers lie around in it
> Broken glass is found in it
> Grass

It wouldn't be pretentious to say that both poems are 'about love' – a particular kind of love, as understood by two very different people. But any ideas about love which the poems generate are sparked off by the particular concrete images of the poems. They are about particular things first, about love second. In the same way, Conrad's novel is about anarchists first, particular individuals in particular situations, and about anarchism second.

It would, of course, be absurd to claim that this effect is universal in imaginative writing. Many successful writers are greatly given to generalising and philosophising, much avant-garde art is specifically concerned with exploring ideas rather than particular situations. Nevertheless, these are more exceptions than the rule, and to begin with at least, it might be useful to forget about thinking about ideas in favour of looking at and writing about things – in your own poem about loved objects, for example. It's bound to be different from Brooke's or Mitchell's, just as your way of looking at the world is different.

What you know

The second assertion about imaginative writing, that you should write from what you know, looks simple enough. But this is not the same as to say that what you write must be true and must have happened directly to you. That would be to confine you to autobiography. There are whole areas which we may not know at first hand but of which we feel we have sufficient intuitive knowledge to write about. A son coming home from war, for instance. Might not a writer who has never experienced war himself be able to write a good short story on this subject? The proof could lie only in the reading of the story itself, in the writer's ability to convince us of the people and the emotions in his story, of exhausted relief, of ecstasy, or (as in Hemingway's 'Soldier's Home', quoted on p.57) of disillusionment and apathy.

Perhaps the most fruitful question to ask is 'do I need to wander out of my own experience?' Your own experience may seem narrow to you, an ordinary family in an average town, a few years at the local school and college, a not unusual job. But all the material is there, even if you want to keep to realistic fiction or drama, ignoring the more purely 'imaginative' world of poetry or experimental prose. According to Flannery O'Conner 'anyone who has survived an average childhood has enough to write about for a dozen years.' That this depends on how you see that childhood, and what you make of it, is implied by her use of the word 'survived'. And the same is true of subsequent periods of your life.

It is characteristic of new writers that they should feel limited by their experience. Partly, this is a result of an uncertain understanding of the writing process, which is as much concerned with transformation of experience as with mere description. But it is also a result of the myths that have grown up around some of the great figures of modern literature. A noted example is the American writer Ernest Hemingway, who believed passionately in the value of violent and intense experience. He made his life revolve around war, big game hunting, deep sea fishing, bullfighting and drinking. This was not only intense living, it was desperate living. Finally the despair overtook him and he shot himself. James Joyce was an expatriate, Kafka died of consumption, D.H. Lawrence lived in Mexico . . . and with somebody else's wife. But Joyce and Lawrence began their lives as schoolteachers, and much of Lawrence's finest writing is based upon the world that he grew up in, the Nottingham mining community. Of Joyce's two most widely read books, *A Portrait of the Artist as a Young Man* and *Dubliners*, the first is almost straight autobiography, the second is a series of sketches of the city he both loved and hated. It's extremely easy to have romantic ideas about unfamiliar places and people, and very tempting to write about them. And it seems to come so easily! It comes so easily, of course, because you're using somebody else's language and material and probably style, and to begin with at least, it's much harder to find your own.

And that's the trouble with the 'exotic' setting. It distracts the writer from the meat of the story, towards the trimmings. In this way it can disguise the true value of the story itself, or the lack of value. Needless to say, this is as true of readers as of writers. It's no accident that a leading publisher of romantic fiction publicises its novels by drawing attention to their settings – love flourishes in tropical islands, historic castles, even (it adds) in the busy atmosphere of a modern hospital. A quick glance at their manufactured plots and cardboard people, and you can see one reason at least why the emphasis is on the setting.

I was once given thirty pages of closely typed manuscript by a foreign student who, it turned out, had once spent a week in Britain. His story was set in England, and turned out to be a threading together of fish and chips, pints of bitter, cream teas, joints of beef, pubs, Stratford-upon-Avon, the river Thames, Trafalgar Square and *Match of the Day*, culminating in a round-Britain cycle race in which the young hero and heroine managed to cycle from Oxford to Liverpool in under two hours. There was obviously a great deal of affection for Britain in his writing, but the results were unfortunate.

'Different from us'

It isn't only beginning writers who fall into this trap, nor is it only romantic settings that lure them, but unfamiliar or inaccessible people and social classes too. Scott Fitzgerald once said in a significant tone of voice to Hemingway: 'The very rich are different from us.' 'Yes,' said Hemingway flatly, 'they have more money.' In our own age, a writer is likely to feel scruples about the social sweep of his fiction. Does it adequately represent the reality of life in a democratic, industrial, multi-racial, pluralist (etc.) society? While these are perhaps important questions to ask, the answer is not necessarily to flesh out your writing to include feminists, merchant bankers, occultists, rock stars, conservationists, oil sheikhs, trade unionists and so on if you happen never to have encountered one of these. You'll probably end up writing an ill-informed essay, not even an ill-informed novel, either because you feel you know it all, or because you don't and feel guilty, and try to hide your ignorance.

A great novelist who strays into a minefield when he moves away from what he knows is E.M. Forster in *Howards End*. In the novel he tries to show, among other things, the divide between social classes and how this might be bridged. He is clearly concerned about this, no doubt also guilty about coming from the privileged upper class which the novel knows and satirises so well. So it becomes necessary to include a character from – The Working Classes! He has one tentative stab. Here it is. Leonard Bast, an insurance clerk, is sitting reading, and painfully 'improving himself', in his basement flat. Jacky, who lives with him, clatters down the stairs.

> 'What ho!' said Leonard, greeting the apparition with much spirit and helping it off with its boa.
>
> Jacky, in husky tones, replied, 'What ho!'
>
> 'Been out?' he asked. The question sounds superfluous, but it cannot have been really, for she answered, 'No,' adding, 'Oh, I am so tired.'
>
> 'You tired?'
>
> 'Eh?'
>
> 'I'm tired,' said he, hanging the boa up.
>
> 'Oh, Len, I am so tired.'
>
> 'I've been to that classical concert I told you about,' said Leonard. 'What's that?'

'I came back as soon as it was over.'

'Anyone been round to our place?' asked Jacky.

'Not that I've seen. I met Mr Cunningham outside, and we passed a few remarks.'

'What, not Mr Cunningham?'

'Yes. Mr Cunningham.'

'I've been out to tea at a lady friend's.'

Her secret being at last given to the world, and the name of the lady friend being even adumbrated, Jacky made no further experiments in the difficult and tiring art of conversation. She never had been a great talker. Even in her photographic days she had relied upon her smile and her figure to attract, and now that she was –

On the shelf,
On the shelf,
Boys, boys, I'm on the shelf,

she was not likely to find her tongue. Occasional bursts of song (of which the above is an example) still issued from her lips, but the spoken word was rare.

She sat down on Leonard's knee, and began to fondle him. She was now a massive woman of thirty-three, and her weight hurt him, but he could not very well say anything. Then she said, 'Is that a book you're reading?' and he said 'That's a book,' and drew it from her unreluctant grasp.

There's everything wrong with this. It's unbelievable (the irrelevant, absurd 'Mr Cunningham' business), it's superior (the opening description of Jacky), it's crude in its humour (Leonard struggling under her 'massive' weight). And the reason is clear. Forster doesn't know his subject from inside, and tries to hide it by turning them into figures of fun. This is a short-term trick, and springs back in his face when he next lets us meet the Basts and expects us to believe in them as important characters in the novel. Here is another novelist, less highly regarded yet in this case as always, keeping to what he knows well, the factories, pubs and terraced streets of Nottingham. The passage is from Alan Sillitoe's *Saturday Night and Sunday Morning*. Arthur, the complacent, womanising hero is standing at a bar. A young woman comes up to buy drinks.

'Have a drink then, duck, while you're here.'

She looked over her shoulder at the others, and, seeing them still talking, said: 'All right. I'll have a shandy if you don't mind. What's that black stuff you're drinking? It looks like treacle.' He told her. 'I've heard of it,' she said. 'I think I tasted it once, but it was too strong.' She sipped her shandy. 'This is as much as I can take.'

'Well, I'm not a boozer either, only I felt like a drink tonight because I've just got back off my fifteen days. A bloke deserves a drink after that.'

'I'll bet he does. What are you in?'

'Army. But I'll be done next year.'

'Shall you be glad?'

'Not much I wain't. I can't get out quick enough.'

'My sister married a man in the air force,' she told him. 'He looked ever so nice in his uniform. He's out now though, and they've got a house up Wollaton. She's expecting a baby next week.'

'Do you live up that way?' he asked, his drink not touched.

'No,' she answered, 'up Broxtowe, on the estate. I like living in them nice new houses. It's a long way from the shops, but there's plenty of fresh air.' He suggested she take the crisps to her family and come back to the bar. 'All right' she said. He heard her say loudly to her mother that she had met a friend from work and wanted to talk to him. He drank.

She returns to him at the bar, and they chat further. Then:

> 'What do you do in the week?' he ventured. 'Do you ever go to't pictures?'
>
> She looked at him with brown suspicious eyes. 'Only on Monday. Why?'
>
> 'That's funny, because I go out on a Monday night as well to't pictures. I allus think Monday's the best night of the week for that sort of thing, because I go for a drink and see my pals at the week-end, and on the other days I have a lot to do, mending my bike, or getting my tackle ready for fishing. And Monday night is allus best for the pictures because the new ones are on then. Which one do you go to?'
>
> 'The Granby.'
>
> 'I go there sometimes on a Monday,' he said, 'and I've never seen you before.'
>
> 'That's because hundreds of other people go as well,' she answered facetiously.

'I'll see you tomorrow night at seven, then,' he said.

'Fast worker, aren't you? All right, but not on the back row.'

'Why not? I can't see unless I sit right on the back row. If I get near the front the picture goes blurred. Something's wrong with my eyes, I suppose.'

'You want glasses,' she said, 'by the sound of it.'

And so it continues. We see the whole pick-up in front of us, and there's not a word or gesture out of place. The curious thing is that, although neither of them is being particularly 'clever' in the things they say or the subjects they talk about, the dialogue holds our attention all the way through, and we do get the sense that both Arthur and Doreen are politicians in the way they manipulate the conversation. A game is being played out in front of us. While it is through Arthur's eyes that we see the situation, and it is he who makes the cynical asides, and introduces the cinema idea, Doreen is evidently quite up to his manipulation.

In Britain at least, what you 'know' about someone has much to do with their social class, and that in turn has much to do with the way they speak. It is class ignorance that trips up Forster, and class knowledge which roots Sillitoe in the immediately believable. Forster has started off with a generalised idea about 'the working class', and tried to create characters to illustrate it. As a result, his scene is not 'rooted in the particular' – which is quite different from Sillitoe's pub conversation, in which he begins with two individuals who happen to be working class. But the scene does not set out to be 'An Illustration of Working Class Life', as Forster's feels it does. Sillitoe obeys, here at least, the two opening maxims of the chapter. He has started with a concrete situation, which is 'rooted in the particular.' And he has written from experience, from 'what he knows'.

What you know best: your own life

The most extreme form of writing about what you know is of course writing directly about your own life in the form of autobiography. Nobody knows your own life better than you do, certainly. But the common response to the idea of autobiography is 'oh, but my life's too boring for anybody else to want to read about it'. Well, two things could perhaps be said by way of a reply to that.

The first would be to make the essential point that it's the treatment you give your material, in this case your life story or a part of it, as much as the interest of your material itself that will make it appeal to the reader (and to you, the writer). The simple fact is that almost all writers inevitably draw directly upon their own lives for their materials. Hemingway's 'Nick Adams' stories and Dylan Thomas's memories of his Welsh boyhood are but two reminders of the fact that childhood, at least, is a domain we all share. Joyce's *A Portrait of the Artist as a Young Man* covers an outwardly uneventful youth, from infancy to the time he leaves university. It begins:

> Once upon a time and a very good time it was there was a moocow coming along the road and this moocow that was coming down along the road met a nicens little boy named baby tuckoo . . .
>
> His father told him that story: his father looked at him through a glass: he had a hairy face.

And it ends:

> April 26: Mother is putting my new secondhand clothes in order. She prays now, she says, that I may learn in my own life and away from home and friends what the heart is and what it feels. Amen. So be it. Welcome, O life! I go to encounter for the millionth time the reality of experience and to forge in the smithy of my soul the uncreated conscience of my race.

In the course of the book Joyce experiments with a marvellous variety of styles each of which captures the exact feeling of each period of his youth.

Perhaps the most enjoyable, and most successful, recent treatment of a writer's own (outwardly uneventful) life is Nick Hornby's *Fever Pitch*. Like most autobiographies, the book is written in chronological order tracing the important events of the author's life – in the case of this author, these happen to be football matches. So Chapter One, for example, is called 'Arsenal v Stoke City 14.9.68', when the love affair began, when the author was eleven, and so it continues to the present. If the book were no more than that, few readers would get beyond the first page. But what the match reports do is provide a framework (and a discipline, a focus) for an unfolding story of a boy's growing up, and his changing relationships with his family, with girls, with other males – and of course football. His absolutely genuinely felt passion for football, and Arsenal in particular, is both reported and reflected upon in a fascinating and hugely entertaining way. (So natural and honest does it all feel that one of the most frequent comments made on his book is 'I could have written that'. But they didn't, of course. What the comment is really saying is 'That book seemed to be about my life'. And when hundreds of thousands of people say that, you have a hit on your hands.)

The second point about writing autobiography that needs to be made is one which is implied throughout this book: namely, that it no longer makes sense to think about the future of a piece of writing only in terms either of publication or of being left to rot in a drawer, as if there was nothing in between. So that if you feel only a limited number of people would be interested in your autobiographical writing, whether by virtue of their locality, or profession or whatever, that shouldn't discourage you in the least. Community bookshops and publishers in particular have been active in publishing both memoirs and creative writing. East London's Centerprise have published two volumes of *Working Lives*, a collection of writing about different trades and occupations by their practitioners in pre-war Hackney.

Nobody can tell you how to write your autobiography. But an example might be of help to isolate one general point concerning technique:

> Pre-1914 in the East End of London – drab to say the least. Two figures walking in the early morning streets. One, a woman dressed in the long dark skirt of the time and a nondescript hat. Around her shoulders a short, black cape, not even of the time, but of some years earlier, for some traces of embroidery still cling to the somewhat rusty coloured surface. Underneath the cape, half hidden by it, the woman carries an armful of newspapers. The other figure is a girl of fourteen, though rather small and childish looking for her age, and together they deliver the papers to various houses and shops until eventually they arrive, as they do every morning, at a door in a back alley-way which is the stage door of the local music hall, the Hackney Empire. They are let in by a man who has evidently been there all night, as he is unshaven and has a muffler round his neck. Actually he is the night watchman and fireman. The three greet each other. They are my father, mother and I. Dad has just reached the stage of making an early morning jug of tea. It is

> hot and strong and we all partake of this exciting refreshment, which is a regular morning event.

This is how Emily Bishop begins 'Embroidery', her contribution to *Working Lives*. The use of the present tense, which gives the effect of an opening cinema shot, is a useful device to help create atmosphere and to give the reader a visual picture. While it is nothing elaborate, it is still a device, and, as such, artificial. It would be a mistake to assume that an autobiography must be free of 'artifice'. Just like anything written, it needs shaping, selecting, and cutting.

As a start, it might be wise to leave a full-scale autobiography for the moment, and try a few chapters about the parts of your life that strike you as the most potentially interesting to write about. Or use them as the basis for some short stories about childhood or growing up. You won't have to worry about sticking to the facts, change them in any way that seems useful, as long as they remain faithful to what you know about. Show them to friends or anybody you know who'd be interested – and this applies to everything you write. It takes time to get over a natural sensitivity, even embarrassment, at having what you've written commented on. But the sooner the better. The next chapter moves from you and what you know to a simple way of creating characters.

IDEAS FOR WRITING

Describe some of the things (you could confine yourself to your own house) which you regard with particular affection, or loathing. Try to avoid telling the reader directly how you feel about them, letting your emotions come through instead in the way you describe the objects.

In a few paragraphs, create a junk shop, or an abandoned loft. Describe the bits and pieces inside, either as a stranger to them, or the proprietor of the shop, or the former owner of the loft, so that some idea of you as a person emerges from the description.

Describe a person, real or fictitious, solely in terms of things. You don't have to be 'factual about them, you could follow a pattern of 'When I think of X I think of . . .'

Minutely describe the sounds you hear going to sleep late at night; or in a fever. Try to capture the sense of drifting into sleep as you describe what you hear.

You wander into a house whose occupants you have never met. Trying to find out what kind of people they are, you go from room to room noting what you see. Describe this.

You enter a strange room in the dark. There are no lights. You have to get to know your way around, and what's in the room, by touch, aided by smell. Describe that process.

Try a description based mostly on images of a few hours at a fairground, or at the seaside, even of a city in the rush hour, or the trivial events you witness on the street below your window.

Make a brief list of some of the events which have been important to you in your life which would be interesting to write about. (Your 21st birthday party may have been important to you, but would not necessarily be right as the subject for a short story.) Childhood, certainly, is full of moments whose significance we only understand after the event. When you have made your list, which itself should prove a useful exercise, select a few and either write them up as chapters of an autobiography, or as short stories. (See 'What you know best: your own life'.)

WHAT TO READ

There is a wealth of fiction that mines the writer's own early life, but here is a short introductory list of some of the best:

Fever Pitch – Nick Hornby
As discussed, a wonderful account of growing up football mad, and of just growing up.

Oranges are not the Only Fruit – Jeanette Winterson
A sharp and touching account of the author's childhood with her Christian Fundamentalist parents.

A Boy's Own Story and *The Beautiful Room is Empty* – Edmund White
A hilarious and poetic memoir of growing up gay in Middle America in the 1950s.

The Bell Jar – Sylvia Plath
A coolly told but quite riveting account of Plath's childhood, breakdowns and suicide attempts.

Empire of the Sun – J G Ballard
How the young Ballard coped with the brutalising effects of war.

Father and Son – Edmund Gosse
An amazingly well observed and compassionate story of the relationship between the writer as a boy and his strictly religious Victorian father.

And When Did You Last See Your Father? – Blake Morrison
Not fiction, but a beautifully realised modern counterpart to the previous book.

And a few masterpieces of writing specifically about childhood:

Paddy Clarke Ha Ha Ha – Roddy Doyle
A technically brilliant and wonderfully sensitive evocation of a small boy's world in working class Dublin, full of competitiveness and vulnerability.

Indian Camp, The Killers and *A Day's Wait* – Ernest Hemingway
Spare, often shocking stories about a small boy's learning the hard way about the ugly facts of life in Thirties America.

My Oedipus Complex – Frank O'Connor
Hilarious story about an Irish boy's jealousy over his mother's new baby.

The Lumber Room and *Shredni Vashtar* – Saki
Short stories. Dark and witty portraits of an Edwardian child's mind.

2 *Finding a voice*

In the beginning stages of writing, it is advisable not only to keep a hold on the concrete world and limit yourself to what you know (chapter 1) but also to limit the area you wish to explore in your writing. Rather than thinking about how to present a group of people in a particular situation, and worrying about the style in which you want to write this, (that is, the kind of voice with which you will speak to the reader), you might usefully restrict yourself to one character, and use their voice – or, in other words, write a monologue.

In a monologue, one person speaks to the reader. That one person is all you need. Of course he or she should be an interesting person, for whatever reason – the way they speak, what they think, or because of something that they've done or want to do. In writing a monologue you won't have to worry about too much else. Not your 'style', because someone else is speaking for you, and as the feeling of natural speech is important in a monologue your mind will be concentrated on the way people speak, which is basic to all writing. You won't be able to indulge in 'literary' turns of phrase that so often make the writer purr and the reader wince – not unless your speaker also happens to be given to literary turns of phrase as well, perhaps something to be avoided for the moment. The question, too, of 'plot', what shall I make happen, will be half dealt with. As is frequently said of drama, 'character is plot'. That can mean many things, but at a simple level, a reader can be made to feel a piece is 'going somewhere' simply by having a character interestingly revealed to him. There are as many possible monologues as there are people in the world, and many possible ways of telling them. For the moment we can define a 'monologue' as a piece in which the narrator's personality provides the main source of interest – as opposed to a 'short story told in the first person', in which we might expect other things (the plot, the setting, the dialogue and so on) to provide this.

This is the opening of Bill Naughton's 'Spiv in Love':

> She was a bit of a drip was old Myra, but absolutely gone on me. If she hadn't have been I don't suppose I'd have looked on the same side of the street she was on, let alone take her out. But I'm like that I am. I can't turn my back on a woman who looks up to me and thinks I am somebody, even if, what you might say, I can't bear the sight of her otherwise. I must admit a bit of the old flannel goes a long way with me, especially if a woman tells me I dress well. I do like anything like that. Another thing I've got to have is a woman around that I can be off-hand with, blow my top with if I feel like it, and generally say what I want to, clean or dirty. Most women won't stand for it, because they ain't got the savvy to see it don't matter, and that once you've said what you want and done what you want, all the best what was underneath is on top. But them dames that can see it can make a bloke feel at home. Not that I like to go regular with that sort of woman – because as a rule they're on the scruffy side, and a bloke can't show 'em off to his mates in the dance hall or in the pubs, which I like to do with a woman – but if they ain't good enough for a steady, I do like to have one on the side as a fill-in.
>
> Although I say it myself as shouldn't, I was dead smart when I first picked up Myra.

And he goes on to tell us in great detail what he was wearing that night. Never mind Myra for the moment. From the start, we are in the Spiv's world, his turns of phrase and tone of voice taking us right into the East End with him. The story goes on, fairly conventionally, to tell us how the spiv kept Myra 'on the side for a fill-in' and finally got a taste of his own medicine. What really holds our interest, though, is the way we find out more and more about the spiv, about his (generally outrageous) attitudes to women, dress and sexual relationships. His character is the mainspring of the plot.

In a short story told in monologue, the character of the narrator is often of overriding interest. The story we read is a glimpse into the narrator's world, and letting the character speak for himself is a very effective way of giving us that glimpse. Such is Muriel Spark's 'You Should Have Seen the Mess', a first person account of a young woman's life in which we are told about her family, her school, her first jobs and so on – but our attention is caught by the apparently irrelevant remarks she keeps making about the tidiness (or more often untidiness) of places she visits and people she meets. This is not some strange clinical obsession but an insight into her humourless and rather priggish soul. She can't see beyond the piles of dust in a room, or the stains on somebody's clothes, but we can, to a fuller, freer world which her cast-iron notions about respectability and order and 'mess' prevent her seeing. This makes it a very funny, and painful, story to read.

Increasingly we feel we are reading two stories, events as seen by the speaker, and events as seen by us. This is a great advantage of the monologue form, and it's great fun to do. The events in themselves don't have to be dramatic: it is the difference between the two ways of seeing them that entertains the reader.

No plot at all

Even in such a short space, a monologue offers many opportunities. You could easily dispense with the idea of plot completely, and just try to let the character *speak*, about something or someone of importance to them. Although a monologue is obviously written, (by you), trying to capture the feel of the speaking voice, its rhythms and digressions, can be a help in convincing the reader of the reality of your character. Now if your character is, say, a model railway enthusiast, that may or may not make for an interesting monologue. If he says the conventional things about model railways then the reader is likely to be bored. But if his talking about model railways can be used to suggest his entire psychology, the way he looks at and deals with the world, then it might be interesting. Or there may be an idea, an event, a possibility, something that the speaker in your monologue thinks about all the time, which differentiates him or her from other people. In the piece opposite, I have imagined a man thinking about death. Obviously this is something that everybody thinks about at some time or other, but here I've tried to show a particular individual getting himself tied up in the ironies and paradoxes of preparing for death. I didn't think it necessary to specify where he lives, what he does for a living, and so on.

> 'Images of that horror'
>
> Ripeness, as when your fingers cleanly strip the skin off a tangerine, no white bits in the fingernails, and the skin falls away

obediently, leaving the perfect fruit bare and ready. The skin, pitted and rubbery, complies with the fingers, can be neatly discarded, that's how it must be.

Today, I trod on a frog. Purely by accident of course, as I was opening the garden gate. Naturally, I put down my briefcase and lifted the frog onto the grass, where it sat quite still, its mottled, leathery sides contracting and expanding, its eyes unblinking, its innards trickling from the split in its rear. The eyes never closed, but the flanks became still. It was a moving, not to say inspiring, sight. I watched it all. No hysteria, no death rattle, just the knowledge that life was slipping out with the brown slime accumulating on the grass, and acceptance. It must have been after a spider, when my heel ended that. But it didn't matter. Animals are like that.

It doesn't scare me, you see. Oh, it used to. But when you think about it, it isn't that which is frightening. My wife used to complain, uneasily I thought, that the Elizabethans were 'so bloody morbid' putting their memento moris everywhere, a skull on a screen, a figure with a scythe on a wooden chest.

I used to be scared, certainly. There was one occasion when we had friends to dinner, including one sweet old lady who was leaving the party early as was her custom. I helped her to the door and she cried 'Oh bless you' and took my wrist in her skinny hands. As she beamed at me, I saw her dry, dying skin draped over her skull, and only two blank sockets where her eyes were, and her teeth bared and mouldy and revolting. When I went back into the dining room, all I was aware of was a bunch of skeletons nodding at each other, their knives and forks clashing on the china, their teeth gnashing at beef. My wife played a very good Lady Macbeth that night, and was exemplary in her handling of the guests.

It was a difficult period and I have to admit she was most understanding. She bore with me while I buried myself in Keats, the Jacobeans, Edgar Allan Poe, anybody who would tell me what I wanted to hear. Shakespeare's Troilus, the fool, obsessed me for a time. I even spent a night in a morgue, and she was patient of all my Gothic habits. There were times when I had to sleep in the spare room, because I couldn't stand the thought of our sacks, as I called them, rubbing together. And she was a greater support than any man might ask his wife to be.

Then I remember driving down the street and seeing a piece of scaffolding narrowly miss an unsuspecting pedestrian. I leapt out of the car, I suppose to see if he was all right, and found myself becoming quite furious with him, shouting at him and shaking him. He was so nonchalant. 'What if it had hit him, would he have been ready.' I shouted. 'Look mate, a miss is as good as a mile, see?' he said, and walked off.

And of course they're all like that. Take Lear for instance. They all go on about the 'birds in a cage business', but the whole thing comes over in the three perfect lines.

Kent Is this the promised end?
Edgar Or image of that horror?
Albany Fall and cease.

Which brings me back to ripeness. The peel falling away from the fruit. Every day I look in the newspapers, and every day I find, a woman waiting to go to the dentist slips off the platform in front of a tube train, her fashionable heel caught in a crack: a man on holiday with his wife eats shellfish and dies, or stumbles during a cliff walk, or drowns in a sudden undertow. (They say that your whole life flashes before you as you drown, an illusion conveniently fostered by scared people.) It's all so appallingly sudden, so unexpected. Few of them know as much as the frog this afternoon. They just don't think, you see. My wife wouldn't think either, she was, in the end, like everyone else, pretend it isn't there. She was all very sympathetic when I was a bit loony, but once I started thinking about actually preparing myself, which is the only thing to do, she moved out. Other men, I've noticed, take new and younger wives.

Not me. I'm like a mountaineer, skilfully defiant but prepared. I have often considered living in San Francisco, that doomed city. It would please me to know that those fine skyscrapers would one day, soon, be split by huge cracks, and tumble, Babylonian, into the sea. But I went there once, and was sickened by the ignorant gaiety of the place. I had hoped that living in that city would be like climbing a mountain.

So instead I live here, and wait. I am ready for that moment. I am ripe.

It isn't much rooted in time and place, but then I think I wanted that. His obsession with being 'prepared' is precisely what keeps him from entering into the here and now. If the character's 'literariness', his quotations, his reading of poetry, is irritating, well, that's an essential part of him too. He's 'refined' all right, and one of the consequences is that he can't shrug his shoulders and get on with living. Instead he reads, broods, and prepares.

This quality of the speaker not being 'all there', in the everyday world, is even stronger in this last piece. Here we have just a few moments of an individual's life, no introduction, no conclusions. It was written by a student of mine, and is untitled.

> The earth is brown. I don't know what kind of brown – one with a lot of yellow ochre mixed in it. It looks stale and worn in the evening sun.
>
> The earth is strewn with flowers. They fall from the tree above me. On the branches of the tree they hang in bunches but on the ground they are all single and separate. They are lemon yellow in colour, but even though the flowers are dead now, the colour is fresh. I like the combination. Red brown ochre and vibrant yellow.
>
> The flowers move restlessly over the ground, like some sleepy old flying carpet from the Arabian nights. All of a sudden they seem to freeze – not actually freeze because the petals vibrate – ever so slightly.
>
> I walk away from the tree; I keep walking and the earth flows beneath my feet. I don't know why people stare so much. The children stare with large eyes, sometimes they laugh – I like the children. The other people look and quickly move their gaze. They try to look into my mind. I hate that. I pity them.
>
> I come to the sea . . . It looks hard, metallic. Like some kind of amalgam. Liquid mercury, sprayed over in parts by platinum that shines coldly.
>
> On the beach there is a barefoot boy selling bubbles. They are very pretty. There are so many of them. I follow one – it floats in the air in starts. Now up, up then down. It is reluctant to come down, touch the sand. It moves parallel to the ground for some distance and then all of a sudden I can't see it anymore.
>
> The boy comes to me. I give him a coin. He gives me a loop like thing in return. It is a metallic wire in a circle with a small handle. I forgot to ask him how to make the bubbles and I cannot spot him now among the people.
>
> The sea seems not to move at all. It is so still.

Admittedly some people find this fairly baffling. We don't know where or how old or what sex the speaker is, why (s)he is there or where s(he) is coming from. But these things aren't the only ones which help us to understand a person. What we do have is a glimpse into a very private world. It is a world of only partial comprehension of what is going on around the character. We can feel that in the way (s)he describes so carefully 'The earth is brown. I don't know what kind of brown . . .' yet so flatly, the details of the physical environment, the earth, the trees, the sea, the boy. The sentences are short, and generally make simple statements. It is as if the character has only a fragile hold on reality. People try to look into the person's mind: 'I hate that. I pity them.' There's something quite beautiful about the character's mental world, the way (s)he *responds* to these physical details, but something eerie too. There's a feeling of a dream about it, as if the reasons why any of these things should be aren't quite clear; but it seems to be the way the speaker always experiences the world. That's one of the great advantages of the monologue form: five minutes' first-hand experience is enough to take us into the whole consciousness of an individual.

These four monologues show a kind of progression along a scale, with at one end something absolutely realistic, with a strong 'social' slant ('Spiv in Love') and at the other something closer to a dream, a strictly private, inaccessible world ('The earth is brown . . .').

'Spiv in love'
A familiar social type perfectly reproduced. Very much 'in the world'

'You Should Have Seen the Mess'
A less easily identifiable social type, with particular obsessions. Interacting with the world in gen eral.

'Images of that horror'
Though obviously an 'educated' man, social position unimportant. His ideas more important than his world.

'The earth is brown . . .'
The private world, not interacting with other people. Impossible to specify the social type, sex, or age of the speaker.

These distinctions are fairly crude – a monologue about an easily recognisable social type could perfectly well suggest a very private world, for instance. But the importance of the social world decreases, roughly speaking, in each story. The more 'private' or 'extraordinary' a person is, the less likely it is that the outside world, as defined and accepted by ordinary people, will play a significant part in their monologue. Assuming that, for the moment, you are primarily interested in looking at one character, rather than telling a full-blown story with a plot and so on, there are of course an infinite number of points along this scale for you to choose from – and no reason why you shouldn't shoot off either end, or make up a different scale of your own. Moreover, as the plot of a story develops and becomes more complex so too does the role of the narrator. Does the narrator know, for example, the whole truth about the events s(he) describes? Might the narrator have a vested interest in seeing things a particular way? This is looked at in more detail in chapter 6, 'Who's telling the story?'

IDEAS FOR WRITING

Write all these in a monologue form.

Imagine a particular place, nothing extraordinary, perhaps someone sitting in the bar of their local waiting for the evening to start, or a music-crazy kid coming out of a rock concert, or someone in the act of doing something, playing darts, cutting the grass, sitting down to write a letter. Tell the reader what is going through their head. Keep it realistic, down-to-earth, thinking about the way your kind of person talks.

Write the thoughts of someone you've often seen, never spoken to, but feel you know. Include the details you know about them, imagine some more of your own. Their thoughts are wandering as they sit on the train or look out of the window.

Something obsesses you – the way your husband, or father comes in from work, the mess your flatmates make, the music from next door, a particular ritual you always go through with somebody, a particular activity you do. At times this obsession dominates your consciousness. Write about one of those times. Let the reader feel the force of that obsession.

You are an extraordinary person or creature in an extraordinary situation. You live at the bottom of a well, or behind a cupboard, you have known all Time, you are a spirit, a saint, a strange character from history. Speak for a few pages, and convince the reader of your existence by doing so.

Use any of the following passages as beginnings for your own monologues. Adapt them in any way you wish.

a) He's in the room below at the moment. He's been there half an hour. I heard him go in there, and I can hear him moving around in there now.

b) As you might imagine, you meet some funny blokes in my line of business. Like the other day, this geezer in a bowler hat flags me down and says 'Buckingham Palace – fast!' 'Oh yeah,' I think, getting into gear and moving off. Half a minute later he jumps up and shouts through the partition 'D'you know what I've got in here?' 'No,' I says, 'I don't. Let me guess'

c) Three minutes to go. That should just be long enough. Take a deep breath. Stop trembling. That's right.

d) The upstairs room in the house opposite, above the one where the geraniums are, often has its blind drawn. Even on a sunny day like this morning. From where I am, I can see the stairs that lead up to that room, and every now and then someone goes up there.

e) Every morning the soldier is there. He knows I'm looking at him, and doesn't like it. He looks about nineteen. He holds his gun as if someone was going to come up and take it away from him.

Some writers specialise in writing in the first person, especially writers of short stories, where (as we saw in this chapter) much of the interest can lie in the unpeeling of the narrator's character. A few good ones:

WHAT TO READ

The Tell-Tale Heart – Edgar Allan Poe
A murder story where the prime source of suspense is the narrator's obsessive psyche.

The Diary of a Nobody – George and Weedon Grossmith
Hilarious picture of a clerk's daily existence in Victorian London where the joke is definitely on the feebly self important Nobody, who tells the story.

Other People – Martin Amis
A brilliant novel narrated by a young woman who has lost her memory and who tries to understand her world from scratch.

Lolita – Vladimir Nabokov
Not the smutty story of popular imagining, but a stunningly clever and witty comic tale, the pleasure of which comes almost entirely from the character of the cynical genius of its narrator, Humbert Humbert.

Last Orders – Graham Swift
One of the best things about this highly praised novel is the way the story (such as it is – about a day trip to Margate) is told by each of the main characters in turn. The result is a unique psychological complexity.

3 Time to talk

Even if you have been quite successful in using someone else's voice in a monologue, you will face a quite new situation when you come to writing a dialogue between two or more people. A character in a monologue follows his own path, decides his own rhythms and areas of interest. In dialogue, each speaker instinctively reacts to the language, personality, social position, sex, tone of voice of the other, and can be seen to be doing so in what he says. The challenge of dialogue is enormous, and crucial: no good extended piece of writing can live without at least some of it, many good pieces (some of Hemingway's short stories, for instance) rely almost solely upon it. However powerful or subtle your writing may be, if you skimp on dialogue you run the risk of losing the feel of independent reality that all good fiction needs. The reader will begin to feel stifled by your personal viewpoint and want a *first-hand* knowledge of the people concerned. Otherwise the characters will remain shadowy and unreal, like people we have heard talked about but never met. For it is in hearing people speak that we get to know them best, or at least form a distinct impression of them, and understand something of the relationship between them.

It's an important feature of the classic nineteenth century novels, by writers like George Eliot, Dickens, Henry James, Tolstoy, Balzac, that they burst at the seams with dialogue. It's no coincidence that they adapt so well to television 'classic serials'. It isn't only that much of the dialogue can be transposed from the page to the screen: it is that a direct result of that wealth of dialogue is vivid, fully imaginable characters. And that makes for good television, good soap opera, and good reading. Why is it that Dickens' characters are such familiar figures on television, cinema, advertising, comic books? Largely because they talk so much, and talk in a highly personal, idiosyncratic way. It's a lot easier to film a Jane Austen novel than a novel like Albert Camus' *The Outsider*. A modern classic such as this is less concerned with characters in the ordinary sense of the word than with the narrator himself as a 'figure' and the ideas that are generated by his conflict with the ordinary world. This is not a failing on Camus' part, of course. It's a different kind of writing. But if you are keen to create a strong sense of the real, various, everyday world, the world out there rather than the one within, then a good measure of dialogue is essential.

Many people believe dialogue to be easy to write. It is. You can cover pages quickly and write exactly in the way people speak. But it won't necessarily be interesting. You have to be selective, letting the reader work on their own to fill in the picture. It isn't merely 'information' that dialogue should be conveying. There are usually more economical ways of getting that across. What a reader needs from dialogue is a sense of two or more people interacting, whether pleading, bargaining, probing, letting out their frustrations, not getting through to each other, being cold, loving, angry, perhaps conscious that what they're saying isn't exactly what they want to say. More than anything else you write, your dialogue has to be alive, has to feel unplanned, spontaneous, not entirely predictable. This is true whoever is speaking, even if they are abnormally articulate. It's often pointed out, for example, that Jane Austen's characters are rather more articulate than people in real life. That's true, but they never merely deliver speeches to each other, they're alert to what is moving below the surface. And if one of them isn't, and through his own conceit or insensitivity is delivering speeches, that quality is always comically present in their contributions to the conversation.

Here's a passage dealing with a fairly familiar situation, the adolescent boy who's fallen in love, and a possessive mother.

> 'Is she so fascinating that you must follow her all that way?' Mrs Morel was bitterly sarcastic. She sat still, with averted face, stroking, with a rhythmic, jerked movement, the black sateen of her apron. It was a movement that hurt Paul to see.
>
> 'I do like her,' he said, 'but –'
>
> '*Like* her!' said Mrs Morel, in the same biting tones 'It seems to me you like nothing and nobody else. There's neither Annie, nor me, nor anyone now for you.'
>
> 'What nonsense, Mother – you know I don't love her – I – I tell you I *don't* love her – she doesn't even walk with my arm, because I don't want her to.'
>
> 'Then why do you fly to her so often!'
>
> 'I *do* like to talk to her – I never said I didn't. But I *don't* love her.'

'Is there nobody else to talk to?'

'Not about the things we talk of. There's lots of things that you're not interested in, that –'

'What things?' Mrs Morel was so intense that Paul began to pant.

'Why – painting – and books. *You* don't care about Herbert Spencer.'

'No,' was the sad reply. 'And *you* won't at my age.'

'Well, but I do now – and Miriam does –'

'And how do you know,' Mrs Morel flashed defiantly, 'that *I* shouldn't? Do you ever try me?'

'But you don't, Mother, you know you don't care whether a picture's decorative or not; you don't care what *manner* it is in.'

'How do you know I don't care? Do you ever try me? Do you ever talk to me about these things, to try?'

'But it's not that that matters to you, Mother, you know it's not.'

'What is it, then – what is it, then, that really matters to me?' she flashed. He knitted his brows with pain.

'You're old, Mother, and we're young.'

He only meant that the interests of her age were not the interests of his. But he realized the moment he had spoken that he had said the wrong thing.

from *Sons and Lovers* by D.H. Lawrence

How is it that dialogue like this manages to be so powerful, even out of context, when dealing with such a common conflict? I once asked a group of students to look at this passage, and they read it with great insight and sensitivity to what was going on, and awareness of the way the writer showed unspoken as well as spoken fears. One student later continued the dialogue herself:

'Yes, I am old. But I tell you I was young once, and I didn't go doing just as I liked. I had some respect for my mother.'

'Well . . . times have changed, mother.'

'A mother's love doesn't change.'

'But I can't stay around here with you all the time. I've got to be with my *own* friends. And I need her to talk to as well. Annie's all right, but Annie's my sister, and I . . .'

'And what's wrong with your sister? She learns art at school, if that's so important to you. Talk to her about Herbert Spencer,

> or whoever he is.'
>
> 'Sisters aren't the same. And besides, everybody else . . .'
>
> 'I don't care about everybody else. I'm your mother, and I don't think any girl can be so marvellous as to take you away from your family day in and day out. And there are plenty of books here for you to read.'
>
> 'No, mother. It isn't the same.'
>
> 'Or the public library.'
>
> Paul shook his head. Mrs Morel raised her voice in anger.
>
> 'Why is it that kids today want it all their own way? We were *happy* to spend time with our family . . . Oh, I don't care. Go to her, if she's so marvellous. Only don't come running to me every five minutes for your bed and board. Let her provide that for you – then we'll see if she's so marvellous.'

And so on. To continue another writer's dialogue, particularly when it comes from the middle of a full-scale novel, is probably not a very worthwhile exercise: arguably the mother and son here become different people when 'scripted' by a different person. But the results are interesting to compare with the original. Does the student's continuation maintain the standard of Lawrence's dialogue? Well, no, sadly. The extraordinary thing about Lawrence's is that although Mrs Morel says some pretty harsh things, which Paul does too in a clumsy way, we pick up quickly that her heart is breaking beneath her aggressive manner. Yet while Paul denies his love for the girl one minute, and uncertainly tries to defend his relationship with her the next, Mrs Morel doesn't let up. She seizes on anything she can, desperately, first with her aggressive 'What things?', then comes back again immediately when Paul seems to have a simple, conclusive answer with 'And how do you know . . . that *I* shouldn't? Do you ever try me?' And this is just after she has given her pathetic but also, we might say, manipulative answer 'No . . . and you won't at my age.' It is in the illogicality of her aggressiveness that we see how frightened she is.

In Lawrence's dialogue the struggle is intense, poignant, above all confused, with a marvellous balance of the classic roles that mother and son play, with the feel of two complex individuals working out where they stand with each other. In the continuation, we have only the former: the dialogue has degenerated into one about the generation gap, a row between any selfish son and any grouchy old mother. No doubt the generation gap was something very close to the student's heart. And surely to Lawrence's too. But so also, to Lawrence, was the mystery of these two particular individuals, and the power of sex, and Mrs Morel's failed marriage, and Paul's uncertainties about the girl, and . . . This is not to sneer at the student. She herself was completely aware that her dialogue lacked any spark: and realised by the time she finished writing that her idea of continuing the dialogue wasn't a very fruitful one. She had been struck by the way the mother and son picked up what the other had just said, challenging, repeating, rejecting, and there are traces of this quality in her own dialogue. Certainly this is better than planning two people's speeches, chopping them up into blocks of a few sentences and distributing them to their respective speakers. Good dialogue must have the illusion of being organic, self-generating.

Keep yourself out

It is normally part of Lawrence's style to be bold in his commentary upon the dialogue, to direct the reader's attention and sympathy. Here in fact he interrupts the dialogue very infrequently, neither with comment nor 'stage directions'. The mention of the mother jerkily stroking her apron, for instance, is a sufficient visual clue to the tension in the air. He takes us inside Paul's mind at the crucial moment to tell us what Paul *means* when he tells his mother that she is old and they are young, but otherwise the argument takes place before us as if it were on stage. This helps to give the dialogue and the characters that feeling of independent life mentioned at the beginning of the chapter, a feeling which is one of the attractions of a well-written play, in which it *seems* there is no writer intervening between us and the characters he has created. (This isn't only because of the 'visual aid' effect of flesh and blood people on the stage: watching a bad play can give you an uncomfortable feeling of a struggle going on between the living actor and the lifeless, stereotyped part he has to play.) It's a result of presenting character entirely through dialogue and action. Writing which won't let the dialogue stand on its own is at best irritating, at worst gives the sense of the writer being more interested in him/herself than what's going on in the story:

> 'But Steve, who'll cook your Christmas dinner?' Maud protested. I forced a weak smile and reminded her that I cooked for the three of us every weekend. But my sister-in-law brushed

LIBRARY, UNIVERSITY OF CHESTER

> by words aside with an imperious sweep of her arm. 'Christmas is different' she pronounced dogmatically. 'If you refuse to bring the children here, Rose will come round and look after you, won't you, Rose?'
>
> Her daughter looked up from her library book. 'If that's what Steve wants,' she replied flatly. 'Of course he does,' Maud said. 'A woman's touch is essential at this time of year.'
>
> My eyes narrowed. 'Why don't you come too?' I ventured craftily.
>
> She folded her arms across her bosom. 'Certainly not,' she boomed. 'My place is in my own home'
>
> I glanced across at Rose but she quickly averted her eyes, embarrassed. She knew as well as I the game her mother was playing.

In this kind of writing (the passage is from a magazine story) nothing is ever said 'straight': Maud 'protests', then 'brushes his words aside with an imperious sweep of her arm', then 'pronounces dogmatically', then 'booms', having first folded her arms across her bosom. The narrator 'forces a weak smile' then 'ventures craftily', with eyes narrowed. The daughter 'replies flatly.' But what has the reader gained by having so many subtleties of expression drawn to his attention? Nothing at all. While there is nothing wrong with what they are saying to each other the fact that this conversation is introducing the central idea of the story (the matchmaking game of the booming, imperious, protesting Maud) seems to have led the author to write this way in an attempt to make the writing more *vivid*. The result though is not a vivid sense of reality but a vivid sense of the writer's notions of his own vocabulary. Try reading five pages of this at a stretch. You can't make dialogue interesting by finding a hundred different words for 'said'.

Compare this with the following passage from Ernest Hemingway's short story 'Hills like White Elephants'. We are told that somewhere in dusty central Spain, a couple are sitting waiting for a train to come in to an almost deserted station.

> The woman brought two glasses of beer and two felt pads. She put the felt pads and the beer glasses on the table and looked at the man and the girl. The girl was looking off at the line of hills. They were white in the sun and the country was brown and dry.

'They look like white elephants,' she said.

'I've never seen one.' The man drank his beer.

'No, you wouldn't have.'

'I might have,' the man said. 'Just because you say I wouldn't have doesn't prove anything.'

The girl looked at the bead curtain. 'They've painted something on it,' she said. 'What does it say?'

'Anis del Toro. It's a drink.'

'Could we try it?'

The man called 'listen' through the curtain. The woman came out from the bar.

'Four reales.'

'We want two Anis del Toros.'

'With water?'

'Do you want it with water;'

'I don't know,' the girl said. 'Is it good with water?'

'It's all right.'

'You want them with water?' asked the woman.

'Yes, with water.'

'It tastes like liquorice,' the girl said and put the glass down.

'That's the way with everything.'

'Yes,' said the girl. 'Everything tastes of liquorice. Especially all the things you've waited so long for, like absinthe.'

'Oh, cut it out.'

'You started it,' the girl said. 'I was being amused. I was having a fine time.'

'Well, let's try and have a fine time.'

'All right. I was trying. I said the mountains looked like white elephants. Wasn't that bright?'

'I wanted to try this new drink. That's all we do, isn't it – look at things and try new drinks?'

'I guess so.'

The girl looked across at the hills.

Apart from the extreme unobtrusiveness of the writer – there's hardly a word which is not spoken directly by the man or the girl – what is striking here is how the conversation remains interesting to the reader despite the fact that they hardly seem to be talking 'about' anything. The tension in the situation appears in the importance the girl attaches to her little comparison, the indifference of the man towards it, their uneasy knowledge of both these things, the rhythms and repetitions and weariness of 'looking at things and trying new drinks.' So that we know that this is a couple who have known each other too long. And all this without a word of reference to the past, simply from the 'feel' of the dialogue.

Words and actions

Apart from the girl looking at the line of hills, there is not a gesture described in the passage above. That's the way Hemingway liked to write, and said so. Obviously, however, what people are doing can be as important as what they're saying. While we don't need to be told every time a woman folds her arms across her bosom, sometimes that gesture may in fact deepen our understanding of what she is saying. I don't think in the magazine story above it does. It simply isn't necessary. Maud's firmness is quite evident enough. But it might if such a gesture of firmness were unusual in the character, or done defensively, or out of social embarrassment. To risk a generalisation, physical gestures or tones of voice don't really need describing if they could be inferred from the dialogue. What follows is an example of words and actions being delicately used together to contribute to a single effect. The central character, Stephen, is visiting his ex-wife to arrange for their daughter to visit him. He expects his daughter to answer the door, but is met by his wife

> She had the advantage of three concrete steps and she glared down at him, waiting for him to speak. He had nothing ready for her.
>
> 'Is . . . is Miranda there?' he said finally. 'I'm a little late,' he added, and taking his chance, advanced up the steps. At the very last moment she stepped aside and opened the door wider.
>
> 'She's upstairs,' she said tonelessly as Stephen tried to squeeze by without touching her. 'We'll go in the big room.' Stephen followed her into the comfortable, unchanging room, lined from floor to ceiling with books he had left behind. In one corner, under its canvas cover, was his grand piano. Stephen ran his hand along its curving edge. Indicating the books he said, 'I must take all these off your hands.'
>
> 'In your own good time,' she said as she poured sherry for him. 'There's no hurry.' Stephen sat down at the piano and lifted the cover.

'Do either of you play it now?' She crossed the room with his glass and stood behind him.

'I never have the time. And Miranda isn't interested now.' He spread his hands over a soft, spacious chord, sustained it with the pedal and listened to it die away.

'Still in tune, then?'

'Yes.' He played more chords, he began to improvise a melody, almost a melody. He could happily forget what he had come for and be left alone to play for an hour or so, his piano.

'I haven't played for over a year,' he said by way of explanation. His wife was over by the door now about to call out to Miranda, and she had to snatch back her breath to say, 'Really? It sounds fine to me.' 'Miranda,' she called 'Miranda, Miranda,' rising and falling in three notes, the third note higher than the first, and trailing away inquisitively. Stephen played the three note tune back, and his wife broke off abruptly. She looked sharply in his direction.

'Very clever.'

'You know you have a musical voice,' said Stephen without irony. She advanced farther into the room.

'Are you still intending to ask Miranda to stay with you?'

Stephen closed the piano and resigned himself to hostilities.

'Have you been working on her then?' She folded her arms.

'She won't go with you. Not alone anyway.'

'There isn't room in the flat for you as well.'

'And thank God there isn't.' Stephen stood up and raised his hand like an Indian chief.

'Let's not,' he said. 'Let's not.' She nodded and returned to the door and called out to their daughter in a steady tone, immune to imitation.

from 'In Between the Sheets' by Ian McEwan

Here, words and actions combine to give a sharp sense of a couple familiar with each other but also extremely tense. Stephen is able to predict, and forestall, a row at the end, though it is his own fondness for the ironic gesture that has nearly caused it. There is a hint of the flirtatious *and* the nostalgic about his picking out the notes of his wife's call on the piano, and his comment on her voice. She pours him sherry but stands behind him at the piano. She is polite to him one moment, breaking off to compliment him on his playing, aggressive to him the next when he tells her there is no room for her in his flat. His going to the piano is both something to do in an awkward moment but also gives him a fleeting promise of relaxation and happiness. Most importantly, they don't sit and talk to each other, both finding things to do while they speak, in the way that anxious people do, but also in the way that a husband and wife might do in their own home. And in this passage, the folding of arms *is* important. It's the wife defensively drawing up battle lines against her husband. She is *expecting* trouble, which is one of the things that makes the situation so tense.

As always, there are no iron rules to be made. As always, you should become aware of how the writers you like go about it – for example in the proportion of dialogue to narrative, in the way they introduce a passage of dialogue, in the extent to which they comment upon what their characters are saying, whether they present conversations in their entirety or merely a few exchanges to give the feel of a situation at a particular time. Two things can perhaps be adopted as provisional resolutions. Firstly, don't aim for total realism at the risk of boring your reader with everyday chat. While it's got to be the kind of thing people might actually say to each other, it doesn't have to be the kind of thing that people say to each other every five minutes. Select, and edit. Secondly, aim in general to keep yourself out of the conversation and give the characters a chance to stand on their own. Readers can infer from straight dialogue much more than might be supposed – and anyway, a reader should have some work to do, whether in guessing people's motives or feelings, or background, or subconsciously predicting the course of events. It's one of the things that makes a reader engage with the material, and makes reading rewarding.

Can you hear me?

One of the features of the passages quoted above is that they all show people in conflict, and in the Lawrence and the Hemingway at least, unable to 'communicate' with each other. Of course, conflict has always been the essence of a good story and it's an important aspect of modern writing, particularly drama, that people's inability to communicate is as important as their ability to do so. We need to consider for a moment what we mean by communicating. Let us say that two (or more) people communicate when they know what they want to say, and say it, and understand what the other person is saying. They can be in the most violent disagreement with each other and still be communicating. We might then say that Lawrence's Paul Morel and his mother are not fully communicating. Their relationship at this stage is far too confused. When Paul says 'You're old mother, and we're young', what he meant is that 'the interests of her age were not the interests of his'. But the effect of his words is disastrous. In the student's continuation, however, it is more a case of two people simply disagreeing about how a son should behave towards his mother. As I mentioned earlier, Jane Austen's characters, drawn from a social class where a high premium was placed on being articulate, generally don't have much trouble expressing themselves. The Russian playwright Chekhov at the turn of the century was among the first to show that what is not said is as valuable as what is. His characters spend a lot of their time on stage not getting through to each other, and much of the audience's interest lies in seeing exactly in what ways and for what reasons they aren't. Reading modern literature very much involves responding to what is going on below the level of actual speech. Why is it so important to the girl, for example, that the man isn't interested in hills looking like white elephants?

Eventually, however, the writer may come to consider the question 'How do I portray through dialogue two people who actually do communicate quite well and are getting through to each other? Perhaps they even love each other!' 'Good' things are notoriously difficult to depict in writing. Good relationships so easily appear sentimental, good people easily appear cardboard saints, like the moral-religious heroines of George Eliot, or superhumanly tolerant, understanding, sympathetic drips. It might be interesting to go back to *Sons and Lovers*, since we have already seen the two central characters clashing. Here we see them in a sort of natural harmony. Mrs Morel has just been out shopping. Paul is at home painting.

> 'Oh!' she sighed, smiling at him from the doorway.
>
> 'My word, you *are* loaded!' he exclaimed, putting down his brush.
>
> 'I am!' she gasped. 'That brazen Annie said she'd meet me. Such a weight!'
>
> She dropped her string bag and her packages on the table.
>
> 'Is the bread done?' she asked, going to the oven.

'The last one is soaking,' he replied. 'You needn't look, I've not forgotten it.'

'Oh, that pot man!' she said, closing the oven door. 'You know what a wretch I've said he was? Well, I don't think he's quite so bad.'

'Don't you?'

The boy was attentive to her. She took off her little black bonnet.

'No. I think he can't make any money – well, it's everybody's cry alike nowadays – and it makes him disagreeable.'

'It would *me*,' said Paul.

'Well, one can't wonder at it. And he let me have – how much do you think he let me have this for?'

She took the dish out of its rag of newspaper, and stood looking on it with joy.

'Show me!' said Paul.

The two stood together gloating over the dish.

'I *love* cornflowers on things,' said Paul.

'Yes, and I thought of the teapot you bought me . . .'

'One and three,' said Paul.

'Fivepence!'

'It's not enough, mother.'

'No. Do you know, I fairly sneaked off with it. But I'd been extravagant, I couldn't afford any more. And he needn't have let me have it if he hadn't wanted to.'

'No, he needn't need he,' said Paul, and the two comforted each other from the fear of having robbed the pot man.

'We c'n have stewed fruit in it,' said Paul.

'Or custard, or a jelly,' said his mother.

'Or radishes and lettuce,' said he.

'Don't forget that bread,' she said, her voice bright with glee.

Paul looked in the oven; tapped the loaf on the base.

'It's done,' he said, giving it to her.

She tapped it also.

'Yes,' she replied, going to unpack her bag. 'Oh, and I'm a wicked extravagant woman. I know I s'll come to want.'

He hopped to her side eagerly, to see her latest extravagance. She unfolded another lump of newspaper and disclosed some roots of pansies and of crimson daisies.

'Four penn'orth!' she moaned.

'How *cheap*!' he cried.

'Yes, but I couldn't afford it *this* week of all weeks.'

'But lovely!' he cried.

'Aren't they!' she exclaimed, giving way to pure joy. 'Paul, look at this yellow one, isn't it – and a face just like an old man!'

'Just!' cried Paul, stooping to sniff. 'And smells that nice! But he's a bit splashed.'

He ran in the scullery, came back with the flannel, and carefully washed the pansy.

'*Now* look at him now he's wet!' he said.

'Yes!' she exclaimed, brimful of satisfaction.

Mrs Morel is half guilty, half triumphant about what she has bought. But her guilt disappears at Paul's excited approval. They share their delight in the pot, the flowers, the baked bread – and each other. They are high on each other's company. They are not talking about their relationship, they are living it. And within the context of the novel they are supporting each other: Mrs Morel's husband would have shown only anger at her extravagance. Most people (particularly British people) don't like talking about how much they like somebody or how much they value their relationship with them. They show it, if at all, in the things they do together, and in their tone of voice. Lawrence captures both these perfectly. The action is wholly spontaneous – Paul is not at all bothered about being interrupted in his painting – and the speech is excited, sentences not even waiting to be finished:

'Paul look at this yellow one, isn't it – and a face just like an old man!'

Paul runs into the scullery, and there is real affection, for the flower but also for his mother, in his '*Now* look at him now he's wet!'

IDEAS FOR WRITING

Write as many of these in straight, uninterrupted dialogue as you can. Each idea describes a situation in which two or more people talk to each other.

Two burglars are making a midnight haul in a country mansion. They begin to disagree about what they should take.

A woman alone in a house answers the telephone to a young man who fancies her daughter and of whom she does not approve. He tries to talk her round.

A small child asks some difficult questions of a grandparent.

A man returns home late. His wife delicately questions him, trying to pick up clues about where he has been and what, if anything, is 'going on'.

A computer dating agency has arranged a meeting between two people. There has been some mistake in the files.

Two ex-lovers bump into each other after some years at a party. Both their new escorts are present and potentially within earshot.

Members of a family discuss a lodger who has been living with them for a few weeks.

Use any of the following passages as beginnings for your own dialogues, or adapt them in any way you wish.

a) 'I want to . . .'
'Yes I know you do.'
'But you won't let me.'
'It's hardly a question of you needing my permission.'

b) 'I suggest you forget about the whole thing.'
The girl looked at her mother.
'Do you?'

c) Brady and the girl looked at each other. There was a long silence.
'Is this it?' she said.

A workman arrives at the door to do some work in a house, work which involves looking around the different rooms to begin with. Write not only the spoken dialogue between the workman and whoever shows him around, but also their thoughts during the conversation.

A mother and son are being interviewed by a local authority official. The mother and son have one way of speaking to the official and another of speaking to each other (in forms of dialect, slang or simply tone of voice).

A one-way conversation: a zoo keeper talks to the animals as he does the rounds.

WHAT TO READ

Most good writers write good dialogue, but some do it exceptionally well. Comic writers tend to rely on dialogue rather more, as dialogue is better suited to the purpose than lengthy narration.

The Commitments, The Snapper and *The Van* – Roddy Doyle
Almost all of Roddy Doyle's trilogy about his Dublin family, the Rabbits is written in dialogue that feels completely everyday but is also sharp and hilarious.

High Fidelity – Nick Hornby
A portrait of a sexual relationship struggling to survive the hero's penchant for collecting obscure records, Hornby's follow up to 'Fever Pitch' has some wonderfully awkward, utterly believable conversations between boyfriend and girlfriend (as well as between record collectors).

A House for Mr Biswas – V S Naipaul
A tragi-comic portrayal of a crowded, frustrating touching family life in the Caribbean, and the efforts of the hero to rise above it. Lots of talk, lots of life.

The Pickwick Papers and *Our Mutual Friend* – Charles Dickens
Dickens' dialogue is always fresh and often hilarious, because his characters are such originals (not to say eccentric).

4 *Writing about people*

Don't tell, show

There is a sense in which it is meaningless to separate writing about people from any other kind of writing. Just as there is no special way to write about cats, or revolutions, or snow, there is no special way to write about people. Some text books frequently exhort you to USE VIVID WORDS as if this were the key to making people 'come alive'. The question to ask is 'come alive for what, and how?' It depends on what you want to 'do' with a character, and that depends on the kind of story you want to write, and the character's role within it. You will not want to describe in detail every waiter who serves your hero a cup of coffee – but if your hero is feeling threatened by the world then to describe the waiter's contemptuous manner may help to create the desired atmosphere of oppression. The description of the waiter is not done for its own sake, but because it makes him play a part in the story. This is the beginning of a murder story

> 'Did you have a good day at work, darling,' said Jeff, in his deep rich voice. Jeff Bridges was tall and well-built. His eyes, a sparkling chocolate brown and his hair, a deep brown with a hint of blond. His wife Jenny, also tall and slender, spoke in her soft and gentle voice. 'Sure. It was swell.' She had soft, curly blond hair and deep sea blue eyes. Jeff and Jenny were attracted to each other as soon as they met. 'How about you, honey?' she asked. 'It was okay,' Jeff replied.

The writer is making a gallant effort to make her characters 'come alive' for the reader, but the question 'come alive for what' has not been thought about. It is quite unnecessary to know what Jeff and Jenny look like, since their only function is to oil the wheels of a complicated whodunnit plot. (They also seem to inhabit a world based on advertising rather than on reality). Here is another opening:

> Krebs went to the war from a Methodist college in Kansas. There is a picture which shows him among his fraternity brothers, all of them wearing exactly the same height and style collar. He enlisted in the Marines in 1917 and did not return to the United States until the second division returned from the Rhine in the summer of 1919.
>
> There is a picture which shows him on the Rhine with two German girls and another corporal. Krebs and the corporal look too big for their uniforms. The German girls are not beautiful. The Rhine does not show in the picture.
>
> By the time Krebs returned to his home town in Oklahoma the greeting of heroes was over. He came back much too late. The men from the town who had been drafted had all been welcomed elaborately on their return. There had been a great deal of hysteria. Now the reaction had set in. People seemed to think it was rather ridiculous for Krebs to be getting back so late, years after the war was over.

There are no 'vivid words' here. Nor is there any description of what Krebs looks like. What Hemingway has done instead is to give us two photographs, both of which show Krebs as an ordinary guy – college fraternity member in one, off-duty soldier in the other. In the second picture, there is a note of awkwardness: 'Krebs and the corporal look too big for their uniforms. The German girls are not beautiful.' This is taken further in the next paragraph. Krebs' return is mistimed. He is an ordinary guy, but he is also a misfit, and that feeling, of being in the wrong place at the wrong time, is what Krebs, and the story 'Soldier's Home', is about. The device of describing two such photographs, before we properly meet Krebs, beautifully and economically places him in a context, and directs our expectations so that we 'read' him in the right way when we do meet him.

One way of making the reader imagine a character in the way you want is to show the character in action, rather than writing a genuine description of them. Even Krebs is doing something in a specific time and place in the photographs described (for instance, posing for a fraternity photograph) which tells the reader about him. This is Dickens in *Great Expectations*:

> My sister had a trenchant way of cutting our bread-and-butter for us, that never varied. First, with her left hand she jammed the loaf hard and fast against her bib – where it sometimes got

> a pin into it, and sometimes a needle, which we afterwards got into our mouths. Then she took some butter (not too much) on a knife and spread it on the loaf, in an apothecary kind of way, as if she were making a plaister – using both sides of the knife with a slapping dexterity, and trimming and moulding the butter off round the crust. Then, she gave the knife a final smart wipe on the edge of the plaister, and then sawed a very thick round off the loaf; which she finally, before separating from the loaf, hewed into two halves, of which Joe got one, and I the other.

We are *shown her* in a visual way, rather than *told about her*. Her way of cutting the bread for her family is far more telling for the reader than a biographical sketch about her. This is not an essay, but drama enacted before us.

This cannot be separated from the points made in the previous chapter about dialogue. There it was suggested that good dialogue gives the reader first-hand experience of the characters in a book. Dialogue after all is only another way of 'writing about people'. And whether a character is doing something or talking to somebody, the reader is being shown rather than told. There will be very many different ways in which you as the writer can comment on your characters, directly or indirectly, or abstain from comment altogether. But comment alone will not make your characters convincing.

Someone you know

It could be that you are interested in writing accounts of people you actually know. This may seem easier, but it poses its own difficulties. When writing fiction, an author (as was particularly evident in the Hemingway story) generally has some idea what he wants to do with a character, and therefore will concentrate on bringing out certain qualities which will be of importance in the work as a whole. This is not so easy when writing a sketch of someone you know. Will you end up with a rather vague, generalised description because you haven't an 'angle', a 'slant', to help you select the relevant details? That 'angle', of course, may emerge once you start writing, and you see which things work on paper. Here is a writer describing someone they see frequently; a character at the local market, Willy the watchmender.

Willy's full height is very nearly five foot. He is quite bald on top and what hair is left round the sides is rather sparse, and white. He has a round pink face and over each eye rests a silver eyebrow that is long overdue tor a trim. His ravaged nicotine stained moustache seems to droop in defeat onto a protruding red bottom lip. As he sits at his stall, his grey shabby jacket clings tightly to his shoulders, and sharply flares out as it reaches his rather global middle. All the time Willy works, he talks, laughs, and tells jokes to the waiting customers around him. This sort of behaviour of Willy's may give a newcomer to the market the impression that Willy's work is very slip-shod. But on the contrary Willy gives a first class service on the spot and charges only a fraction of what the large high street jewellers charge. Not only that, all the entertainment is free. He will give a running commentary at times of just what is wrong with the watch and what he intends doing about it, and what he is doing at the moment.

'Yes,' he will start, as he removes the back of the watch. 'Yes, the pallet's a bit sticky. Hello, your balance is a bit loose an' all.'

Willy's head would be well down now, his eyeglass buried into the socket of his eye, as his face wrinkles around it. His shoulders well up almost touching his ears, as he probes deep into the recesses of the timepiece. His head and shoulders still firmly in the working position. 'Not been cleaned for months 'as it?' Willy would enquire reprimandingly. While the owner shamefully shakes his head.

If you are alert enough you will notice that Willy's head will at frequent intervals make sudden two second dives under the stall. He will usually make this dive just after a joke has been told and everyone is overcome with hilarious laughter, or he may wait until some other distraction takes place. Willy usually comes up smacking his lips or burping.

But be warned. It is no good going to Willy with a repair if you are in a hurry. For it seems that Willy gives talking and diving priority over watch repairing.

Most customers have been going to Willy for years, and they are like old friends. He will hand a repaired watch back to its owner. 'Firty bob George'.

'Firty bob,' George would reply in mock surprise, as he addresses the audience, and holds the watch up to view. 'Look at that, he only cleaned the bleeding fing. Feiving old git, it's daylight robbery that's what it is. Not coming here no bleeding more.' . . . This fresh bit of excitement gives Willy another opportunity for one of his quick and crafty dives, for the audience are now turned towards the departing customer. On becoming upright Willy burps and selects a watch from one of the dozen that are held out towards him. He gives the timepiece the usual shake and puts it to one of his red ears. His brow wrinkles and his eyes disappear under the silvery brows. In seconds the watch is in a thousand pieces on Willy's table. And the poor nervestruck owner looks on as Willy holds the smallest of screws in his tweezers, and rocks with convulsive laughter at a joke he has just told the audience. Everyone in the crowd is thoroughly enjoying ail this, except of course the poor apprehensive looking fellow who owns the watch. Gradually Willy calms down, the audience too, and the poor nervous chap becomes a little more relaxed. Willy's head goes down, his shoulders move upwards, his face wrinkles round his eyeglass. Suddenly he hesitates, straightens up, takes out the eyeglass and looks questioningly at the tweezers.

He looks back at the audience, then back at the tweezers. He looks back at the audience, and back at the tweezers again.

'It's gorn,' he announces. 'It's gorn.'

The poor panic stricken owner was seen to go completely livid as his trembling white hands clasped each other, and the audience joined in a mass search of Willy's stall. Here was yet another opportunity for a quick dive. And Willy didn't miss it.

Ron Barnes, from *Hackney Writers' Workshop Vol. I*

Willy is presented to us in action, a chaotic, quick-witted king of his market patch. There are plenty of marvellous details (his reprimanding manner with his terrified customers, the shoulders up to the ears with concentration), but two things in particular stick out. One is the short but telling physical description, including the 'silver eyebrow long overdue for a trim' which gives Willy a touch of the wild and devilish. The other is what I think is the best detail of all, because so extraordinary and individual – the dives under the table for a quick nip. It's the kind of thing that has sharp visual impact on the reader, and Ron Barnes seems to have known this, as it forms the central 'theme' the 'angle', almost, in the sketch: whenever there is an event which distracts attention, down he goes. It's often the quick brush stroke of a character in action rather than the painstaking detail that makes a character real. The portrait is a vivid one also because we have to guess what Willy is actually doing in his 'dives' – nowhere are we actually told. The writer is only reporting what he sees – he is showing, not telling, and the result, an element of detective work for the reader, is very satisfying.

Characters in action

Returning to fiction, here is a famous literary walk:

> Two young men came down the hill of Rutland Square. One of them was just bringing a long monologue to a close. The other, who walked on the verge of the path and was at times obliged to step in to the road, owing to his companion's rudeness, wore an amused, listening face. He was squat and ruddy. A yachting cap was shoved far back from his forehead, and the narrative to which he listened made constant waves of expression break forth over his face from the corners of his nose and eyes and mouth. Little jets of wheezing laughter followed one another out of his convulsed body. His eyes, twinkling with cunning enjoyment, glanced at every moment towards his companion's face. Once or twice he rearranged the light waterproof which he had slung over one shoulder in toreador fashion. His breeches, his white rubber shoes, and his jauntily slung waterproof expressed youth. But his figure fell into rotundity at the waist, his hair was scant and grey, and his face, when the waves of expression had passed over it, had a ravaged look.
>
> 'Well! . . . That takes the biscuit!'
>
> His voice seemed winnowed of vigour; and to enforce his words he added with humour:
>
> 'That takes the solitary, unique, and, if I may so call it, recherché biscuit!'
>
> He became serious and silent when he had said this.

The two characters are introduced in the middle of an everyday action: the story concerns the mean, loveless friendship between the two men-about-town. One is holding forth with confidence, even rudeness, the other nervously approves and flatters. So the two men are shown in active relationship to each other, they are placed in a context which defines them: that one talks and the other listens. As he listens he has to bob deferentially on and off the pavement. He has an appearance of joviality and youth, but his face reveals him to be 'ravaged'. He isn't entirely sure when his friend has finished telling his story. His comment is a straightforward piece of boot-licking, and as if he knew it he digs around for something more positive, more 'clever' to say – and adds the clumsy and affected 'That takes the solitary, unique and if I may so call it, recherché biscuit.' This only makes him look a bigger fool than he already feels. 'He became serious and silent when he said this.' His nervousness, his insecurity, run right through this short description.

While 'introduce characters in action' may be a fairly useful guideline, it certainly isn't an infallible one – which of course is true of any 'rule' about writing. In the same stunning collection of short stories, *Dubliners*, Joyce does something quite different. He uses another quite common device, that of introducing the central character by first describing the room in which he lives, whose objects, arranged with immaculate tidiness, tell us a great deal about the man. At other times a writer may deliberately want to keep a character shadowy, rather than vivid. The enigmatic figure of Kurtz in Joseph Conrad's 'Heart of Darkness' is an example. He is a character about whom the narrator hears extraordinary tales, and about whom he thinks obsessively, so that when the narrator and the reader finally meet Kurtz he has become as much an idea or symbol as an actual person.

Detectives, dreamers, outlaws

The previous sentence brings us back to the opening point of the chapter, that what matters is not merely to make a character 'come alive', but to think about the question 'come alive for what, and how?' In the examples we have looked at so far, the writer has wanted to make the reader believe in the tangible existence of his characters. In this sense, he has adopted a *realistic* approach to writing. Kurtz, however, is perhaps more important as an 'idea', of an educated European being taken over by the primitive forces of the remote heart of Africa, than he is as an individual person. It is the shadowy area between people-as-real-individuals, and people-as-ideas, that is the subject of this final section.

The notion of a person being other than a 'real individual' may seem a strange one. But there is a sense in which many people have a power over our imaginations, and therefore a kind of *imaginative* reality: Napoleon, for example, or Billy the Kid, or Marilyn Monroe, (not to mention our own husbands, or girlfriends) exist in our imaginations as strongly as they did in history. And there is much creative enjoyment to be got from exploring this 'imaginative reality'.

In 1935 the South American writer Jorge Luis Borges published his first book, called *A Universal History of Infamy*. Despite its imposing title the book was in fact a little collection of biographical sketches of obscure or infamous villains of world history. The sketches had titles like 'The Dread Redeemer, Lazarus Morell', and 'The Widow Ching, Lady Pirate' or 'The Insulting Master of Etiquette, Kotsuke no Suke.' Borges wrote them for his own entertainment, doing a minimum of research into his subjects and inventing or cooking the facts when it suited him, a trick for which he has subsequently become famous. He wasn't attempting to write history, but to select some details from a colourful figure's life, and the ideas that these gave rise to, and the scenes they enabled him to imagine, and then in five or six pages string these together and bring these characters to life. The material facts of their lives he uses like putty, and he doesn't hide it, speculating on what a character might have thought at a particular moment, effecting rapid scene changes, chopping up the time sequence, and above all presenting the villain's life in a series of brightly-lit scenes.

This is Borges setting the scene for one of his best-known villains.

> History (which, like certain film directors, proceeds by a series of abrupt images) now puts forward the image of a danger-filled saloon, located – as if on the high seas – out in the heart of the all-powerful desert. The time, a blustery night of the year 1873; the place, the Staked Plains of New Mexico. All around, the land is almost uncannily flat and bare, but the sky, with its storm-piled clouds and moon, is full of fissured cavities and mountains. There are a cow's skull, the howl and the eyes of coyotes in the shadows, trim horses, and from the saloon an elongated patch of light. Inside, leaning over the bar, a group of strapping but tired men drink a liquor that warms them for a fight; at the same time, they make a great show of large silver coins bearing a serpent and an eagle. A drunk croons to himself, poker-faced. Among the men are several who speak a language with many s's, which must be Spanish, for those who

> speak it are looked down on. Bill Harrigan, the red-topped tenement rat, stands among the drinkers. He has downed a couple of aguardientes and thinks of asking for one more, maybe because he hasn't a cent left. He is somewhat overwhelmed by these men of the desert. He sees them as imposing, boisterous, happy, and hatefully wise in the handling of wild cattle and big horses. All at once there is dead silence, ignored only by the voice of the drunk, singing out of tune. Someone has come in – a big, burly Mexican, with the face of an old Indian squaw. He is endowed with an immense sombrero and with a pair of six-guns at his side. In awkward English, he wishes a good evening to all the gringo sons of bitches who are drinking. Nobody takes up the challenge. Bill asks who he is, and they whisper to him, in fear, that the Dago – that is, the Diego – is Belisario Villagran, from Chihuahua. At once, there is a resounding blast. Sheltered by that wall of tall men, Bill has fired at the intruder. The glass drops from Villagrans's hand; then the man himself drops. He does not need another bullet. Without deigning to glance at the showy dead man, Bill picks up his end of the conversation. 'Is that so?' he drawled. 'Well, I'm Billy the Kid, from New York.' The drunk goes on singing, unheeded.

Borges comments 'Out of that lucky blast (at the age of fourteen), Billy the Kid the hero was born, and the furtive Bill Harrigan died.' All the tales in this little book have this marvellously strong visual side to them. He also uses bogus 'eye-witness accounts', obituaries, scraps of letters, links with significant historical events, all to give an extraordinary yet light-hearted air of authenticity. He takes chances, but gets away with them.

It's an entertaining and fruitful exercise to flip through a standard encyclopaedia, looking at entries about people, preferably largely unknown to you and the public, decide upon one that interests you, tinker with the facts if you like, throw in a bit of local or historical colour (don't worry if your knowledge of the time and place isn't perfect – think of the New Mexico saloon), select a few scenes you find interesting, and you have your biographical sketch. You'd be advised, however, like Borges, to do it for your own amusement, to flex your muscles in story telling and literary selection, rather than trying to write what blurbs call 'a penetrating study.' But you will be pleased with what you come up with. Obviously it will be better to choose a character who led a fairly exciting life – an explorer, a criminal, a soldier, a prophet. The entry that follows is the fruit of a five-minute scan through *Everyman's Encyclopaedia* (Vol 6: Norsemen – Precious Stones).

> PINKERTON, Allan (1819–84). US detective, born in Glasgow, Scotland. He emigrated to Chicago, where he established the agency which bears his name. He was appointed to the US secret service in 1861, and was prominent in many celebrated cases, assisting in the break-up of the Molly Maguires, a secret society which terrorised the coal districts of Pennsylvania for some 15 years before 1877. Later he was employed as special detective on the great US railways. He published several detective stories, in which his exploits were narrated.

This is the bread and butter of romance. Restless Glaswegian arrives in the New World to find a society perpetually on the edge of anarchy . . . watches a sheriff one day shoot two petty outlaws dead in a bar, only to be shot in the back by another . . . this horrifies the reactionary young man with its waste of resources of law enforcement, which are furthermore so crude that they allow the powers behind crime (which history tells him is bound to become more organised) to escape unnoticed. His Presbyterian (perhaps) background inclines him towards the business élite, who readily supply him with his first contracts. His hatred of the terrorist, Catholic-inspired Molly Maguires leads him on a fifteen year hunt to wipe them out, and the establishment adores him for it. But he has also fallen fatally in love with the imagery of detection, the secrecy and deception and voyeurism, a love which he indulges in his sensational detective stories, in which he shamelessly glamourises his own role. This same love is the cause of his returning to ride the rails across the heart of the lawless American interior, etc, etc, etc.

To make the point once more, this is the Pinkerton of fiction, images and ideas, rather than the Pinkerton of historical fact. I have no idea whether Pinkerton was Presbyterian; but I would certainly enjoy imagining he was, and pulling the threads of the story together on this assumption, and writing scenes which describe the bar room fight, or quoting imaginary extracts from his stories, or describing one journey on the Union Pacific Railway in which Pinkerton in disguise spies on both the passengers and his own detective.

A further encyclopaedia entry, the life of Palissy, an enameller and writer of fantastic stories of 16th century France, appears in the 'Ideas for Writing' section which follows.

IDEAS FOR WRITING

Write a brief sketch of someone (you don't as the writer have to be in possession of many facts) by describing some of the pictures in their photographic album.

Describe someone's room in great detail, with a view to letting the reader know what they are like without having yet met them.

Describe someone in terms of their walk, not forgetting that where they are walking, where they might be going, what they are wearing are as important as their physical movements.

Describe a character as seen through the eyes of a child – a favourite uncle, the mother's lover, a teacher, a family friend, a doctor. You don't need to write in the child's language though your observations must be limited to those a child might make, and indirectly using some of the child's words.

You can see, but you cannot hear, two people having a conversation of enormous importance and interest to you. You are watching them from a window, or spying on them from behind a rock. Describe what you see in terms of gestures, movements, facial expressions, and your own guesses about what they *could* be saying.

Describe a person whom you see frequently (along the lines of Ron Barnes's portrait of Willy) on the street, on the bus, at work, and try to bring out a few of their gestures which strike you as typical or strange. Don't pretend to be anything more than an observer of a real person. You don't *know* the character, you've only watched them.

Using the same, or a similar, character, write a brief biography of that person, making up all the details about their childhood, married life, occupation, fears and so on. The novelist H.E. Bates frequently used to do this on trains, only to be alarmed by how accurate his fictional biographies turned out to be when he began talking to his subjects.

'The first time I met Mrs Enderby, she was . . .' Use this as a starting point for a brief portrait of Mrs Enderby, in which you describe a typical action or situation which conveys something essential about her.

In the role of a frequent visitor, describe the essential images of a group of people, such as a family, a group of students sharing a flat, an office, concentrating on the feeling of the group as a whole rather than the individuals in it.

Mime-in-words. Every kind of person smokes a cigarette, takes off a coat, or makes a cup of tea differently from another. Choose one of these actions, and describe three or four kinds of people doing them. No dialogue, only actions.

Finally, a second entry in *Everyman's Encyclopaedia* Vol. 6, (Norsemen – Precious Stones). Use it as a basis for a fictional biography. This is a man with an obsession:

> PALISSY, Bernard (c.1510 – c.1590). French potter and enameller, born near Agen. His reputation is largely based on literary sources, beginning with his own fantastic writings, according to which he laboured for years in direst poverty to discover how to make fine enamels. Between 1548 and 1563 Palissy succeeded in producing that distinctive ware called by his name, earthenware moulded in high relief with life-like water creatures, shells, fishes, lizards, leaves and other natural objects, and covered with coloured lead-glazes of wonderful harmonies. He escaped the Massacre of St Bartholomew's Day, but with the persecutions of 1586 Palissy was imprisoned in the Bastille, where he died four years later.

5 *Doing things with places*

Student: OK, places.
Writer: Places?
Student: Yes. How to write about them.
Writer: Well, it depends what you want to do with them.
Student: Do with them? Why, make them come alive of course, get up off the paper, feel like I'm there, you know.
Writer: But what about people?
Student: People? Look, I want to know about places, and you're talking about people. I'll put the people in later. Right now I want some atmosphere. That's the reason I want to know about places. Besides, places are interesting aren't they? You always find writers going on about places – Hardy's Wessex, Dicken's London, Faulkner's —
Writer: Right. Now let's think about it.

There's a fair amount of thinking to be done. Yes, places are interesting and places in literature equally so, though they are more interesting than the single word atmosphere might suggest. Certainly atmosphere in a story is important. Remember the advertisement for the publisher of romantic fiction which reminds you that love can flourish in ancient castles, sun-drenched beaches or the busy atmosphere of a modern hospital? They know what they're talking about. Not, incidentally, that the atmosphere of a story and its setting are exactly the same. In the story 'Hills Like White Elephants', part of which is quoted on page 47, the atmosphere of stagnation and futility obviously comes more from the nature of the dialogue than from the location. But the setting, of the dusty, deserted train station in central Spain, as the couple wait for a connection certainly contributes to that effect.

The student above certainly would not be alone in finding an enormous appeal in say, Hardy's Wessex, where a geographical area is marvellously recreated from intimate knowledge. But it is Hardy's sympathy for its inhabitants which gives his knowledge of the countryside such force in his writing. The two are always seen in some kind of relationship. So the student's confident assertion that he'll 'put the people in later' gives cause for alarm. Certainly, pulp romantic or adventure fiction does just that. Thrillers are often set in 'exciting Hong Kong', or New York, or Monte Carlo. Here the atmosphere is just one of the separate ingredients that go to make up the successful formula. The settings could be, often are, switched around without it making much difference. But good writing instinctively recognises the subtle relationships that always exist between people and the places and situations they inhabit, so that this chapter is going to be more about those relationships. Because as the writer says, it depends on what you want to do with them.

Setting the scene

Even the most straightforward use of setting should be more than the frilly ornamentation of the fiction described above. The way in which you write about the place in which your story happens can positively contribute to the mood or ideas of the story itself. Dickens' *Bleak House* concerns a lawsuit which drags on for years, and the lawyers and crooks who profit by it. Dickens begins his novel with a long description of the fog that swirls through the streets of London, then narrows his focus to the Inns of Court:

> The raw afternoon is rawest, and the dense fog is densest, and the muddy streets muddiest, near that leaden-headed old obstruction, appropriate ornament for the threshold of a leaden-headed old corporation: Temple Bar. And hard by Temple Bar, in Lincoln's Inn Hall, at the very heart of the fog, sits the Lord High Chancellor in his High Court of Chancery.

Before the tale even begins to unfold, the reader has a strong sense of gloom and confusion, subsequently strengthened by what happens in the novel.

It is of course possible to bring the relationship between event and place, between what happens and where it happens, even closer so that the setting becomes an important part of the story itself, almost like an extra character. In a story like Ian McEwan's 'Psychopolis,' quoted below, the characters and the setting (Los Angeles) are inseparable. It is a story about barrenness and body-worship and luxury and anxiety and moral decay. The narrator is both attracted and repelled by the city's glamorous-looking boredom:

> It was exhilarating, at least at first, to live in a city of narcissists. On my second or third day I followed George's directions and walked to the beach. It was noon. A million stark, primitive figurines lay scattered on the fine, pale, yellow sand till they were swallowed up, north and south, in a haze of heat and pollution. Nothing moved but the sluggish giant waves in the distance, and the silence was awesome. Near where I stood on the very edge of the beach were different kinds of parallel bars, empty and stark, their crude geometry marked by silence. Not even the sound of the waves reached me, no voices, the whole city lay dreaming. As I began walking towards the ocean there were soft murmurs nearby, and it was as if I overheard a sleep-talker. I saw a man move his hand, spreading his fingers more firmly against the sand to catch the sun. An icebox without its lid stood like a gravestone at the head of a prostrate woman. I peeped inside as I passed and saw empty beercans and a packet of orange cheese floating in water. Now that I was moving among them I noticed how far apart each solitary sunbather was. It seemed to take minutes to walk from one to another. A trick of perspective had made me think they were jammed together. I noticed too how beautiful the women were, their brown limbs spread like starfish; and how many healthy old men there were with gnarled muscular bodies. The spectacle of this common intent exhilarated me and for the first time in my life I too urgently wished to be brown-skinned, brown-faced, so that when I smiled my teeth would flash white. I took off my trousers and shirt, spread my towel and lay down on my back thinking, I shall be free, I shall change beyond all recognition. But within minutes I was hot and restless, I longed to open my eyes. I ran into the ocean and swam out to where a few people were treading water and waiting for an especially huge wave to dash them to the shore.

The awful directionless characters in the story are both producers and products of their extraordinary city. The story is about people, there is a plot but it's also about a place, the two existing in inextricable relationship. And because it's about L.A. with its freeways and luxury and sunshine and private houses, it's about an

American ideal, and because it's about an American ideal it's about – well, it's about a society rather than just a place.

An Englishman's home

In the chapter 'Writing about people' it was mentioned that one of the ways in which a character can be described is by writing about something which belongs to them, most obviously, of course, their home or their room or their lodgings. Depending on how this is done, it can tell us much that the author wants us to know about their habits, personality, income, social class, taste, marriage, and so on. It is worth remarking that the general habit of lengthy description has declined in writing of this century, partly because prose style in general tends to be more economical, partly also because literature has become more absorbed in psychological reality, at the expense of describing the physical details of a society. Tom Wolfe, the American 'New Journalist', points out that the nineteenth-century novelists always gave the reader plenty of clues as to their characters' position in society, their 'status life.' He quotes Balzac introducing two rather hard-up social climbers, whose status life we can read from:

> The furniture covered in faded cotton velvet, the plaster statuettes masquerading as Florentine bronzes, the clumsily carved painted chandelier with its candle rings of molded glass, the carpet, a bargain whose low price was explained too late by the quantity of cotton in it, which was now visible to the naked eye.

Wolfe goes on to say that this function of minute social categorisation has now been taken over by the so-called New Journalism, which blends fiction and documentary.

It isn't only status life that can be conveyed by the meticulous description of someone's house, but also emotional life – and again we are back to atmosphere, but again it's atmosphere with a purpose. There is a marvellous, lengthy description in Brigid Brophy's novel *Flesh*, of the mock-Tudor suburban mansion owned by the parents of the main character, Marcus, as seen through his eyes. The more we know of Marcus' parents' house, and the smell of furniture polish and the neat 'hostel' bedroom, and 'the terrible pitch of cleanliness at which Marcus' mother kept all fifteen rooms', the more we share the character's sense of oppression in his family home, oppression mixed with a sense of relief at being warm and secure after his dingy flat. Of course, we learn too about his parents' 'status life', about affluent bourgeois mock-Tudor respectability and so on. But it is its emotional reality for Marcus that is the striking thing.

Mental landscape

The Victorian John Ruskin wrote 'All violent feelings . . . produce in us a falseness in all our impressions of external things, which I would generally characterise as the "Pathetic Fallacy"' – 'pathetic' because it concerns feelings, fallacy because our view of things when we are violently emotional is distorted. A fallacy it may be in strict physiological terms, but as far as writing goes, to link emotion with the world outside is a powerful and much-used way of conveying an emotional state of mind. To give a simple example, a lover's joy is made more real for the reader when set in a beautiful place on a sunny day. The external world is frequently used to reflect the inner world of the individual. In a sense, of course, this is a part of the basic process of writing, using images to show the reader, rather than tell them about, an experience.

In Saul Bellow's first novel, *The Victim*, the hero Leventhal is on his way to an unpleasant meeting:

> After a hurried supper of a sandwich and a bottle of soda at a stand near the ferry, Leventhal crossed to Staten Island. He walked onto the deck with his hands in the pockets of his fully buttoned, wrinkled jacket. His white shoes were soiled. Posted beside a life ring, his dark forehead shining faintly under his ill-combed, thick hair, he gazed out on the water with an appearance of composure; he did not look as burdened as he felt. The formless, working, yellowish-green water was dull, the gulls steered back and forth, the boat crept forward into the glare. A barge was spraying orange paint over the hull of a freighter, which pointed high, lifting its bow out of the slow, thick cloud. Surely the sun was no hotter in any Singapore or Surabaya, on the chains, plates, and rails of ships anchored there. A tanker, sea-bound, went across the ferry's course, and Leventhal stared after it, picturing the engine room; it was terrible, he imagined, on a day like this, the men nearly naked in the shaft alley as the

> huge thing rolled in a sweat of oil, the engines laboring. Each turn must be like a repeated strain on the hearts and ribs of the wipers, there near the keel, beneath the water. The towers on the shore rose up in huge blocks, scorched, smoky, gray, and bare white where the sun was direct upon them. The notion brushed Leventhal's mind that the light over them and over the water was akin to the yellow revealed in the slit of the eye of a wild animal, say a lion, something inhuman that didn't care about anything human and yet was implanted in every human being too, one speck of it, and formed a part of him that responded to the heat and the glare, exhausting as these were, or even to freezing, salty things, harsh things, all things difficult to stand. The Jersey shore, yellow, tawny, and flat, appeared on the right. The Statue of Liberty rose and traveled backwards again; in the trembling air, it was black, a twist of black that stood up like smoke. Stray planks and water-logged, foundering crates washed back in the boat's swell.

Had Leventhal just fallen in love, could he have reacted in the same way to the crossing? Would he have had such sympathy for the men in the shaft alley? Because he is 'burdened' the whole scene strikes him as oppressive, the water is 'formless, working, yellowish-green', the boat 'creeps forward into the glare'. What is surely the most impressive piece of mental landscaping in the passage though is Leventhal's likening of the light on the tower blocks and on the water to 'the yellow revealed in the slit of the eye of a wild animal, say a lion, something inhuman and yet . . . implanted in every human being too'. What a sinister image, and yet how naturally it comes from the Manhattan skyline, filtered through Leventhal's tormented consciousness.

However suggestive of other things this light is, it is still palpably real light on a real river. In H.G. Wells' short story 'The Door In The Wall', a place is described which reveals things about the personality of the main character, but whose existence remains deliberately ambiguous. Wallace, a successful politician talks one night in the club to an old friend, and tells him in some desperation of a secret that has been haunting him since he was a child. When he was about six years old and playing alone he had passed a door in the wall on the street, and felt a strong desire to go in. He had done so and stepped into a garden of unspeakable beauty and 'friendliness'. He had been overwhelmed by the emotion of joy it moved in him.

Circumstances prevent him returning to the garden and when he does try to find it again, he can't. In later life he sees the door in the wall on several occasions, but always at a time when politics are pressing him to move on. 'Who wants to pat panthers on the way to dinner with pretty women and distinguished men?' Finally he realises he has lost something of infinitely greater value to him than the world he has chosen.

Wallace's garden is representative of an inner place which he has destroyed to his cost. It is a symbol of the child-like and innocent in him. Obviously, places can be symbolic of areas of experience. Perhaps the greatest exponent of this technique is Franz Kafka, whose method is to create bizarre or fantastic situations and describe them in matter-of-fact, realistic detail, so that we are wholly convinced of, for example, the reality of his symbolic castle, in the novel of the same name, in which the central character tries repeatedly and unsuccessfully to gain admission; or of the dingy corridors of the law courts in *The Trial* where justice is endlessly talked about, but with no apparent logic or urgency. So real are the places in these novels, despite their evidently metaphoric purpose in the book, that people frequently talk, when describing the oppressiveness of a bureaucratic procedure, of a 'Kafkaesque atmosphere'. And again we are back to our starting point, atmosphere.

The simple point that all these extracts have in common is that while the setting may be important in each, it is always a part of the purpose of the story or sketch as a whole. Places exist in relationship with people. The use a writer makes of place arises from the ideas and emotions of the work itself.

The diagram below may help to bring together in visual form the possible 'uses of place' that have been discussed in this chapter.

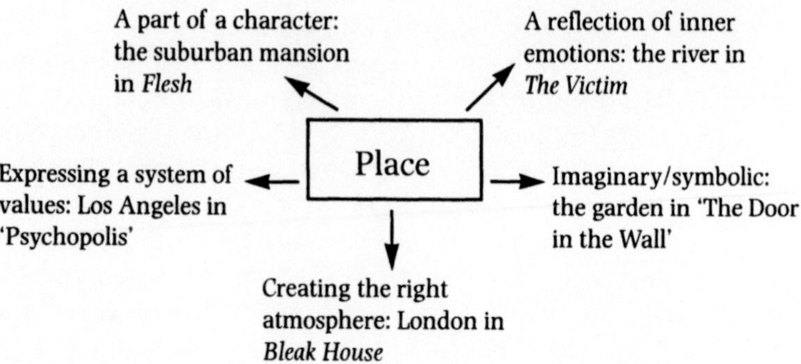

WHAT TO READ

Some good evocations of place in nineteenth and twentieth century fiction:

Waterland – Graham Swift
A stunning novel about history and personal memory which uses the East Anglian fens – flat, bleak, inscrutable – as an integral part of the unfolding story.
Snow Falling on Cedars – David Guterson
A vivid evocation of life in the fishing and farming community of an island off the north west coast of America, and a murder that happens within it.

Tess of the D'Urbevilles and *The Woodlanders* – Thomas Hardy
As with all books that use their setting well, the life of the people who make their living there is just as important to Hardy as the natural surroundings. But Hardy also knows better than anybody how to use place to enhance the drama of a story.

London Fields – Martin Amis
Of course it isn't only natural surroundings that bring atmosphere and depth to a story. Amis's London (Notting Hill in particular) is a (sometimes darkly) comic world of seedy pubs, bedsits, porn shops, take aways, and the people who make their living in them.

The Riddle of the Sands – Erskine Childers
This marine spy thriller from the early twentieth century is a tale of stealthy observation and secret pursuits in the sandbanks and shoals off the Friesian islands off the German coast. A gripping story, it is also fantastically atmospheric.

6 *Who's telling the story?*

In writing any piece of fiction, the question of who is to tell the story needs to be thought about. Is it to be you, the author, who knows everything about all the people and all the events in the story? Or is it to be one of your characters, describing what happens to him or her? Are there more ways than just these two to tell a story? The answer to the last question is yes. This chapter looks at the range of possibilities available to you, and the advantages and drawbacks of each.

The three most common ways are:

a) in the third person, where you the writer tell the story

b) in the first person, where the narration is done by one of the characters

c) in the third person, with the focus on one character, from whose point of view the events are related.

The third person The writer tells the story directly, and does not pretend to be anything other than the teller of the tale. This is how Tolstoy begins Anna Karenina:

> All happy families are alike but an unhappy family is unhappy after its own fashion.
>
> Everything had gone wrong in the Oblonsky household. The wife had found out about her husband's relationship with their former French governess and announced that she could not go on living in the same house with him.

That it is the writer who is telling his readers the story is reinforced by the confident generalisation with which the story opens: 'All happy families . . .'. There is no doubt that the writer is in control. And Tolstoy goes on to tell us in this lengthy novel not only about the Oblonskys, but the Karenins, and Levin and Vronsky, all of whom he can tell us about with the same intimate knowledge.

It is because it is assumed that the author knows everything about his characters that this technique of telling the story is known as that of the 'omniscient author'. At first glance, it may seem that the freer you are the better, so why not go straight for this third person narrative, which puts you in complete control of the characters and the action and which allows you to go anywhere you like? But there is a snag in being the omniscient author, which is that all stories need a focus, and constantly having the responsibility for where you place that focus (the responsibility which is always yours as the omniscient author) can be quite a strain. Put simply, how many of the characters' thoughts and actions are you going to describe and which characters are you going to focus on? The freedom of the third person technique brings with it the need always to make decisions of this kind.

The first person If we look at a different style of narrative technique, writing in the first person, we find different constraints and possibilities. A character in the story (usually, but not always, the main character) speaks to the reader. Here is another opening from a nineteenth century Russian classic, Dostoevsky's *Notes from Underground*:

> I am a sick man . . . I am an angry man. I am an unattractive man. I think there is something wrong with my liver. But I don't understand the least thing about my illness, and I don't know for certain what part of me is affected. I am not having any treatment for it, and never have had, although I have a great respect for medicine, and for doctors. I am besides extremely superstitious, if only in having such respect for medicine. (I am well educated enough not to be superstitious, but superstitious I am.) No, I refuse treatment out of spite.

This is not the writer speaking, but his strange, 'underground man.' The 'focus' is immediately clear, as it is provided by the character who is telling the story. Whereas in third person narrative we have the problem of what to include, and what to leave out, at least with the first person we can only include what our central character has experienced. Simply, he cannot be in two places at once. Nor can he know what other people are thinking, though he can have ideas about it, which may or may not be right. So the path is at least cleared of some choices, in a way that is probably useful to a beginning writer.

The other advantages of the first person technique have already been dealt with in 'Finding a voice' – that the question of the style you write in is made simpler for you because you have to keep to the voice of your narrator, and that this will prevent you from indulging in 'literariness', or at least agonising over the style in which you want to write. It also provides immediacy: this happened to me, I'm telling it to you, which is the most basic form of story telling.

The third person with the focus on a single character It is the writer who actually tells the story, but he centres it on one character only, so that the story is that character's, but the writer can draw back if he wishes, to make a comment or tell the reader about what someone else in the story is doing. In this passage, Arthur, the hero of Alan Sillitoe's *Saturday Night and Sunday Morning* is having a drink with Jack, who is the husband of Brenda, the woman who features in Arthur's thoughts.

> Arthur watched him, thankful that certain laws existed to prevent you from seeing into each other's mind, that things were marvellous that way.
>
> 'It don't mek no bit o' difference,' the barkeeper insisted, 'not wi' fifty bloody transfers.'
>
> 'What about Worrel and Jackson? You can't say they wain't mek any difference.'
>
> Arthur listened in a dreamlike way, happy from the beer he had drunk, dimly remembering the cold earth of the dark wood where he had lain with Brenda, hours ago: he had heard all about football before.
>
> He reflected, fingering what he decided would have to be his last pint if he were not to begin a real bout and fall into a hedge-bottom on the way home, that it was just Jack's bad luck. Either you had it in for you, or you didn't. He told himself that he would make the best of it, stack hay while the sun shone. Brenda was a good woman to know, and he wouldn't stop until things cracked up, as they must, he didn't doubt, sometime, one way or another.

Although there is no pretence that anyone other than the writer is telling the story, still the convention is observed that he can only describe what is going on in one character's head, as if, like Arthur, the writer accepted that 'certain laws existed to prevent you from seeing into each other's mind.' In this way, much of the helpful discipline of first-person narrative is retained.

Just how helpful that discipline can be is exemplified by some remarks that E.M. Forster made while writing his novel *A Passage to India*.

> I am bored by the tiresomeness and conventionalities of fiction-form: e.g. the convention that one must view the action through the mind of one of the characters; and say of the others 'perhaps they thought', or at all events adopt their view point for a moment only. If you can pretend you can get inside one character, why not pretend it about all the characters?

But Forster himself immediately supplies the answer to that question:

> 'I see why. The illusion of life may vanish, and the author degenerate into a showman.'

To 'degenerate into a showman' is to treat your characters like puppets, whizzing in and out of everybody's thoughts, rather than limiting your point of view to the partial understanding which is the most any of us can ever have. It is not that writing in the third person must inevitably degenerate into showmanship, simply that the other techniques keep a useful check on you.

Although attention is focused on one character with this narrative mode, and the plot is built around them, the author is free to establish some distance between himself and the character if he so wishes, or even imply criticism. A totally perfect hero or heroine would be a bit of a bore. There can be a range of attitudes towards the main character. Jane Austen described her Emma as 'a heroine whom no one but myself will much like', and while Emma is at root selfish and immature, her wit and liveliness make her attractive to be with. Alan Sillitoe has a certain affection for his Arthur, the hero of *Saturday Night and Sunday Morning*, but shows his insensitivity without hesitation. What we respond to in Arthur is not his morals but his vitality. We enjoy his company. This, too, is part of the 'illusion of life' that good writing has. Writing fiction is much more about creating this illusion than of having a superhuman knowledge of mankind. How you tell your story, or who you tell it through, or who tells it for you, will be a major factor in achieving it.

The best of both worlds?

You may, of course, wish to experiment by using more than one technique at a time, for instance by writing part in the third person and the rest in the first. That does present difficulties in that the 'illusion' is broken. What *is* quite common is to include letters, diary extracts and so on, written by characters in a book which is otherwise told in the third person. This provides the immediacy, and the feeling of objectivity, of the first-hand account, and gives the reader a clear view of a character as they express themselves. The author meanwhile keeps the freedom the third person technique gives him. Or two versions of reality can be played off against each other: John Fowles' *The Collector* is the story of how a repressed, mean, self-pitying young man who has come into a lot of money kidnaps a self-confident and beautiful middle-class girl and keeps her in a specially prepared cellar. The first part of the book is narrated by the young man, the second consists of the diary the girl keeps while she is a prisoner. The interest lies obviously in the relationship between the two views of what is happening.

Or you can write about a character seen through the eyes of another. In the first few pages of Herman Melville's 'Bartleby the Scrivener', a story about a silent, exasperating, sinister petty clerk, the narrator, Bartleby's employer, introduces himself thus:

> I am a man who, from his youth upwards, has been filled with a profound conviction that the easiest way of life is the best. Hence, though I belong to a profession proverbially energetic and nervous, even to turbulence, at times, yet nothing of that sort have I ever suffered to invade my peace. I am one of those unambitious lawyers who never addresses a jury, or in any way draws down public applause; but, in the cool tranquillity of a snug retreat, do a snug business among rich men's bonds, and mortgages, and title-deeds. All who know me, consider me an eminently safe man. The late John Jacob Astor, a personage little given to poetic enthusiasm, had no hesitation in pronouncing my first grand point to be prudence; my next, method. I do not speak it in vanity, but simply record the fact, that I was not unemployed in my profession by the late John Jacob Astor; a name which, I admit, I love to repeat; for it hath a rounded and orbicular sound to it, and rings like unto bullion. I will freely add, that I was not insensible to the late John Jacob Astor's good opinion.

We form the impression of a man who is complacent, pompous and perfectly satisfied with the world and himself. The reader is bound to ask how far such a person can be trusted to understand the tortured, enigmatic soul of Bartleby.

Representing another variation on 'straight' narration, many of Henry James' short stories concern events which are narrated by people at three or four removes from the events themselves, via people who have their own ideas about the significance of those events. Whose is the right story? Nobody's. It's the spaces between that matter most. Paul Scott does this over a vast area in his *Raj Quartet*, set in India, in which an unspecified shadowy narrator strings together a story with diary entries, conversations with people twenty years after the event, official memoranda, club registers, unpublished memoirs, letters, reminiscences and so on to build up a vastly complicated picture of India around the time of independence.

In the next chapter, a short piece of work by a student who tinkers with the question of who is telling the story is examined in detail.

IDEAS FOR WRITING

Write a possible opening scene for a short story, in which, say, someone is waiting to meet their estranged wife or husband, in two ways: in the third person, with you the writer describing whatever you think important to the scene, and then in the first person, so that we have only your own thoughts as you wait.

A short story in letters only – letters to and from, say, four or five people, allowing the plot to develop through the letters. Some possible situations: a soldier abroad writes home, but he is changing, and so is home; an administrative error in a big hospital leads to a baby being given to the wrong mother, with complicated consequences, including a possible cover-up attempt; letters to a problem page, the internal memos that circulate round the magazine office, a mistake or two, and the printed replies.

A short story in which it emerges that your narrator does not fully understand what is going on in the story, because he has misunderstood something said to him, or because he lacks the sensitivity to see what is really happening.

You recall an important scene in your family history (a death, an unpopular marriage, a large and unexpected gift of money), which took place when you were an adolescent. Compare your impression of this with a diary which you then find in the loft, in which the writer (grandparent, sister, cousin, brother-in-law) describes that event in detail as it was happening. It could, of course, also be your own diary that you find.

Write the opening scene of a story in which a character is talking about an experience they have had. Try to make the reader gradually aware that you do not necessarily share your character's views – but remember that they are doing all the talking. (See also 'Finding a voice': the stories 'Spiv in Love' and 'You Should Have Seen the Mess').

This is the beginning of Edgar Allan Poe's classic horror story 'The Tell-tale Heart';

> TRUE! – nervous – very, very dreadfully nervous I had been and am; but why will you say that I am mad? The disease had sharpened my senses – not destroyed – not dulled them. Above all was the sense of hearing acute. I heard all things in the heaven and in the earth. I heard many things in hell. How, then, am I mad? Hearken! and observe how healthily – how calmly I can tell you the whole story.
>
> It is impossible to say how first the idea entered my brain; but once conceived, it haunted me day and night. Object there was none. Passion there was none. I loved the old man. He had never wronged me. He had never given me insult. For his gold I had no desire. I think it was his eye! yes, it was this! He had the eye of a vulture – a pale blue eye, with a film over it. Whenever it fell upon me, my blood ran cold; and so by degrees – very gradually – I made up my mind to take the life of the old man, and thus rid myself of the eye forever.

It is evident that he is a madman, despite his protestations. Write a story in which the narrator is disturbed in some way, so that we are never entirely sure of the 'truth' of what he is saying.

7 Who's telling the story? – second time around

This chapter looks at one very short story in the making. The story does raise some questions about 'point of view' – but with all kinds of creative writing, it is impossible to talk about a piece only in terms of one aspect. The story, written by a student, is interesting for other reasons, such as the style the writer uses and the revisions she makes after the first draft.

A story that tells of a relationship between two people, particularly of a sexual or emotional kind, where sometimes it can be hard to tell where one person stops and the other begins, provides a useful starting point for examining narrative viewpoint or angle. You can devote a whole book to it, as John Fowles does in *The Collector*, or you can try and tackle it in a sketch as the student does here. Can there be such a thing as the correct view of a relationship? Should you just concentrate on one side? But then what about the other partner? Don't they get a look in? Perhaps you could let one of them describe the whole thing, but make it clear that you sympathise with the other (as in 'Spiv in Love' quoted in 'Finding a voice').

In the story below, about a husband and wife, the writer uses the common third person narration with the focus on one character, referring to the husband as 'he' but viewing the relationship through only his eyes. We learn in two ways about the couple, through the husband's thoughts and through the dialogue. What do we learn about the wife, and how?

'Funeral' (First draft)

'The woman has died in me,' he thought.

'And now her corpse pleads for our sake . . .'

Soon the gold would bite his guilt.

He hated fuss at funerals. He knew this would go on and on and on.

'Why don't you tell me if there is another woman?' 'I'll understand.'

'You can make me understand.' 'But please don't, you musn't . . .'

He knew he wasn't expected to speak or explain. Only listen and feel sorry. For her?

'But what went wrong? Tell me that at least! I didn't even know you were thinking all these things, all this while. Talk to me!'

He thought of the ultimate in road signs. Stop. Finish explanations. Proceed.

'I'm fed up of railway compartments,' he began quietly.

'But what's that got to do with our marriage?'

'I'm entitled to leave and travel allowance. And maternity leave for my wife. I drink coffee from a pot in the office. At home I make do with a mug.'

His eyes were fixed on her tee-shirt. He needn't look at her face to read her. The tee-shirt revealed all. Right now it flashed, 'Stop confusing me you bastard.'

'Talk sense will you? We've been married two and a half years. And now all you can talk of is trains and maternity money.'

If he weren't so drained already he'd have gone across and hugged her. He wasn't sure how she'd interpret that.

'Do you want me to go to my mother's for a few days? I know I can get on your nerves sometimes. I can always manage to go to work from there.'

Toss. Grope. Catch. The quick-and-easy century.

He thought of solutions in cans and test-tube tomorrows when he made love to her that night.

Next morning she felt alright.

'Why had he made love to her?' he asked himself.

No, he didn't regret it. As always he felt good about it. He couldn't figure out why. 'I have rejected her, haven't I? Am I using her?

Or . . . am I paying back a debt? What debt?'

No use denying he didn't feel guilty about all this. But this way, this could go on endlessly. 'How do I bury the corpse with the minimum of ceremony?'

She thought of last night. 'Yes it's all over. The trouble has blown over.' Her confidence made her a woman again.

'Have you checked the alarm?' she asked him after dinner next night.

'I didn't hear it ring this morning. About last night . . . I want to . . .'

'Forget last night.'

'I just wanted to say how . . .'

'Cut the symbolism from last night. There wasn't any.' He knew what she was fumbling over . . . How can a marriage die without explanations?

He wondered if he were the corpse himself. Would it be easier burying him?

He thought of his managing director's secretary. She was leaving after 23 years with the company. There wasn't a single typewriter in the whole office she hadn't used and passed on to the newcomers.

Who is she? Does she know? She's all glass and reflection. Too dazzling for comfort. Too expensive for day-to-day consumption. My wife.

Scratch me out of yourself, wife. Do it now. Or you'll be dead.

The husband's impressions (he is an interesting analyst of his own feelings: 'Toss. Grope. Catch. The quick-and-easy-century') contrast with his inarticulate complaints, and his wife's helpful suggestions ('Do you want me to go to my mother's for a few days?'). But when we get to the sentence half way through 'The next morning she felt alright', we face a problem. Is this something being told us through the husband's consciousness? Is that just what he thought? If so, nothing has changed. But soon we read 'She too thought of last night. 'Yes it's all over. The trouble has blown over.' Her confidence made her a woman again.' This strikes the reader as puzzling because it is inconsistent. So far the writer has concentrated on the man's perceptions – now we are let into the woman's mind. But only for a moment. Back to the man, up to the final 'Scratch me out of yourself, wife.' It is as if the door has suddenly been opened on to the wife and then slammed shut. Better to have left it locked, and let the reader enjoy speculating about what was behind it. What's more, that brief reaction, 'The trouble has blown over', because they made love the previous night, is a rather stereotyped one, and the woman instead of remaining simply unknown to us, becomes a stereotype too.

A diagram might illustrate the problem. Everything inside the triangle is the story:

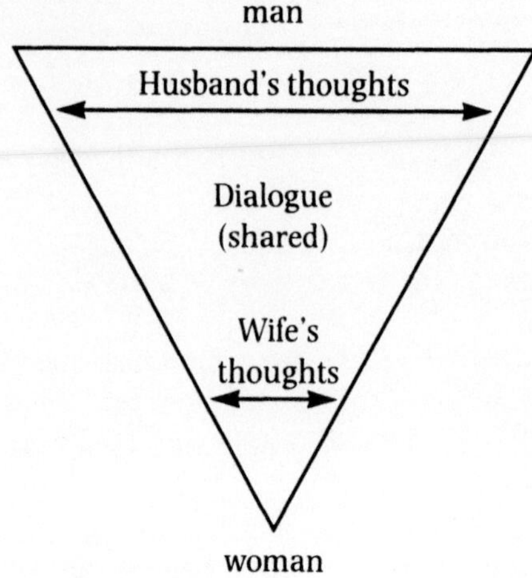

The imbalance is obvious: if we are to know any of the wife's thoughts, let us know them all, or we will feel the full side of her story has been withheld. Alternatively, let us know only the man's, and be left to work out the woman for ourselves.

The criticism was made, the writer thought about it. In the next version she looks at her first draft again before moving on to the second, and finds much she wants to change, and cut:

'Funeral' (first-draft, with student's comments)

'The woman has died in me,' he thought.

arty 'And now her corpse pleads for our sake . . .

~~Soon the gold would bite his guilt~~

He hated fuss at funerals. He knew this would go on and on and on.

'Why don't you tell me if there is another woman?' 'I'll understand.' 'You can make me understand.' 'But please don't, you musn't . . .'

adds nothing ~~He knew he wasn't expected to speak or explain. Only listen and feel sorry. For her?~~

~~'But what went wrong? Tell me that at least! I didn't even know you were thinking all these things, all this while, Talk to me!'~~

He thought of the ultimate in road signs. Stop. Finish explanations. Proceed.

revise

'I'm fed up of railway compartments,' he began quietly.

'But what's that got to do with our marriage?'

'I'm entitled to leave and travel allowance. And maternity leave for my wife. I drink coffee from a pot in the office. At home I make do with a mug.'

all too clever

~~His eyes were fixed on her tee shirt. He didn't look at her face to read her. The tee shirt revealed all. Right now it flashed, 'Stop confusing me you bastard.'~~

~~'Talk sense will you? We've been married two and a half years. And now all you can talk of is trains and maternity money.'~~

complicate things

~~If he weren't so drained already he'd have gone across and hugged her. He wasn't sure how she'd interpret that.~~

too obvious

'Do you want me to go to my mother's for a few days? ~~I know I can get on your nerves sometimes.~~ I can always manage to go to work from there.'

Toss. Grope. Catch. The quick-and-easy century.

too arty

He thought of solutions in cans and test-tube tomorrows when he made love to her that night. *more about the woman here??*

Next morning she felt alright.

irrelevant

~~'Why had he made love to her?' he asked himself.~~

~~No, he didn't regret it. As always he felt good about it. He couldn't figure out why. 'I have rejected her, haven't I? Am I using her?~~

~~Or . . . am I paying back a debt? What debt?'~~

~~No use denying he didn't feel guilty about all this. But this way, this could go on endlessly. 'How do I bury the corpse with the minimum of ceremony?'~~

She thought of last night. 'Yes it's all over. The trouble has blown over.' Her confidence made her a woman again. *expand*

put later

'Have you checked the alarm?' she asked him after dinner next night.

'I didn't hear it ring this morning. About last night . . . I want to . . .'

YUK!

~~'Forget last night.'~~

~~'I just wanted to say how . . .'~~

~~'Cut the symbolism from last night. There wasn't any.' He knew what she was fumbling over . . . How can a marriage die without explanation?~~

pushing the funeral idea a bit far?

He wondered if he were the corpse himself. Would it be easier burying him?

He thought of his managing director's secretary. She was

leaving after 23 years with the company. There wasn't a single typewriter in the whole office she hadn't used and passed on to the newcomers.

too slick!

~~Who is she? Does she know? She's all glass and reflection. Too dazzling for comfort. Too expensive for day to day consumption. My wife.~~

weak ending

~~Scratch me out of yourself, wife. Do it now. Or you'll be dead.~~

Another conversation needed - about going to the pictures? The woman is too shadowy in the story - or should she be out of it altogether? She is a stereotype, tho'. That's why the hub. is fed up with her. The conversation, and some of her thoughts, could show that, maybe.

She has cut a great deal; significantly, and quite rightly, it is the slick, self-conscious writing that goes first: 'Too expensive for day to day comfort. My wife.' Some of the shakier dialogue is cut, too: the rambling about coffee in pots or mugs and maternity leave, and the American B-movie-type 'Cut the symbolism from last night. There wasn't any.' A few notes are made, that what we know of the wife is unsatisfactorily told. The problem is that the wife is meant to be a 'stereotype' of a woman anyway. 'That's why the hub. is fed up with her,' the writer notes. She wonders how to make this clear. The fruits of her painstaking approach, and her willingness to cut a large proportion on her own initiative, are shown in the second, final draft.

Funeral (Final draft)

'The woman has died in me,' he thought.

And now her corpse pleads 'for our sake . . .'

He hated fuss at funerals. He knew somehow that this one would go on and on and on.

'Why don't you tell me if there is another woman? I'll understand. I can help. You can get over it. After all a marriage is stronger than any other woman, isn't it?'

He thought of the ultimate in road signs. Stop. Finish explanations. Proceed.

'I'm fed up of railway compartments.' He began quietly. 'I'm bothered about the way I can make you do just about anything.'

'But that's surely not a crisis. Tell me what's wrong. Can't you talk seriously. Do you want me to go to my mother's for a few days? I can get to work from there. You can have dinner next door.'

Toss. Grope. Catch. The quick-and-easy century. He thought of solutions in cans and 'hit and miss marriages' when he made love to her that night.

Why did he do that? There's somebody who has been sleeping next to me for two years. She happens to be my wife. Is that a good enough reason? I'm not even sure what makes her tick. What she feels deep inside, whether she knows she has an inside. And I say I don't care . . . then why?

She thought things were okay next morning. His silence was unnerving. But she let it pass. She planned on buying tickets for the evening show and then calling him at her office. An evening out would do him good, she thought.

'I'm married,' he kept telling himself in between his memos, and letters and phone calls and coffee.

I have a ready-made wife. A company flat. A credit card. And still the blank wall day after day.

He didn't mean to be offensive when he asked her to go to the movie by herself.

She was home before him. The tea was ready.

'You wanted me to go for a six o'clock show alone? Did you figure out how I would get back? What if somebody saw me leaving the theatre alone? I could get picked up you know. Do you ever wonder what it is like to be a woman?'

He wondered if she knew. He wondered if her mother knew. Or his mother for that matter. He wondered what they felt when they got their periods every month. He had asked her once and she had stared at him.

He kept thinking of his secretary. She was leaving after 23 years with the company. There wasn't a single typewriter in the whole office she hadn't used and passed on to newcomers. He wondered what typewriters felt staying in the place so long.

'We have to go next door for dinner tomorrow. It's the little one's birthday. Should we take a present?'

'You decide.'

'I think we'll buy him a shirt. Blue suits him fine. Don't forget to check the alarm. I don't think I heard it ring this morning.'

He wondered if he were the corpse himself.

Should he start believing in life after death?

She has kept the best of the husband's enigmatic thoughts – cricket, road signs, typewriters. The story has been tightened up, and the melodrama of 'Stop confusing me you bastard' or 'Am I using her? Or . . . am I paying back a debt? What debt?' gives way to something bleaker – the incomprehension about periods and the time he had asked her, the apathy of 'He wondered what typewriters felt staying in the place so long.' But rather than eliminate the thoughts of the wife she has increased them. She tells us not only that the wife was relieved the morning after love-making, but that she had plans to improve the relationship by organising a trip to the cinema. The proportion of dialogue to the man's thoughts is increased too, so that we learn more about her that way too. But the story remains the husband's. It is his thoughts that are interesting, his language that is special. The wife occupies a bigger area of the triangle, but the imbalance is still there. Critics talk in elaborate ways about 'artistic structure', but it often comes down to something like this – a feeling of proportion. Either a story such as this is about 'a relationship seen from the husband's point of view' with dialogue to complement that, or it is a view of both sides, as in *The Collector*, where the space between the two people's versions is of enormous importance. 'Funeral' doesn't quite manage to avoid falling between these two stools.

It should be said at some stage that for the story really to take off, it should be rather longer so that our knowledge of the relationship is deepened. As it stands, though, it succeeds quite well in capturing a mood, of bleakness and apathy. The solution of our immediate problem is not hard to see. If the paragraph which begins 'She thought things were okay next morning' were cut out altogether, then the wife would remain 'unknown' to us. We know about the husband, we know about the dialogue, what is going on in the wife's mind is up to us to guess. And – this is both one of the pleasures and one of the fundamental principles of creative writing – there don't have to be any right answers. In 'Funeral' we know all that it is generally given to one person to know in reality. And that makes for 'the illusion of life'.

8 *The world from the inside*

Follow your thoughts

At the end of the chapter 'Finding a voice', about writing monologues, it was clear that we were moving away from anything simply definable as a character sketch, or a story told by one person, and towards something I called then a 'meditation'. In this, an intensely private world was being created, with its own private images and rhythms, suggesting an individual consciousness relating to what is immediately around it. If you are writing a story you are bound to some extent by the need to get your plot moving – even though an enormous amount of your plot may spring from the development of a character. But if you are interested in short, experimental pieces, you may not be so interested in plot, or even in character. You may want to push language to the limits you can take it, in an effort to explore that mysterious personal world we all inhabit, but which the demands of social living rarely allow us to communicate. You sit looking out of the window, or lean against a bus stop in the queue, or let your attention wander as someone speaks to you, or watch the pattern the streetlamps make on the cement. Instead of forcing yourself back to 'reality', you follow your thoughts for a few minutes.

This meditation simply takes a feeling as its starting point, a feeling that something is about to happen.

> 'Emergence'
>
> Yesterday I felt something straining inside me. The dream that had lain so passive in its womb was outgrowing it. And I felt the strain.
>
> There is this tree I've always seen. It's beyond the neighbour's wall. Sitting upon it, the other day, I happened to notice how the root had insidiously crept half into the wall. Now every day I hold my breath and look out for the ultimate shattering of plaster that will leave the bricks bare, exposed. The wall is tense.
>
> I've felt the frantic convulsions of the earth as the sun tries

to push itself out, and seen it bursting at the seams . . . and held my breath. And the cloud, I can hear its lining slowly being ripped open, and wait . . . for the stitches of rain to fall apart.

Looking at the sea, a blue ache in the distant afternoon sun, always makes my eyes seem blue too. Achingly blue. So blue that they could be the eyes of the sea. And the ache inside them, the ache of the sea – so deep that the sea walks with me. On the road. And sees – the man and the woman on my left and right walk beside me. The man with his left foot first, the woman with her right. And me, I can't really decide. It's difficult whichever way I do, we're not going to be together all of us. I'd like it. It looks good, feels good. To have rhythm. I try to have it. Keep shuffling. And reshuffling. Finally it works.

I have this weight on me. It's massive. But I feel like the mountain – its shoulders sagging under the weight of clouds.

You see, I must, I have to rhyme with everything, and everything, just everything has to rhyme with me. Like when I write this, the skin on my knuckles flexes to jerk my fingers up and down and the letters emerge. Even a scrawl is rhythmic! Rhyming with the dream.

Now out, grown, emerged, rhymed. This.

When first she read this to a group of fellow students, the response was a request to hear it again. And then again. Even then, several people criticised it because they felt baffled. And it did prove impossible to paraphrase. But that could be something in its favour: if it were paraphrasable, if it could simply be 'put into other words', then the unique private quality of the piece would be lost. It is the essence of private experience that it resists this process – which isn't to say that it can't be communicated. It is true that she uses words in an idiosyncratic way: 'Looking at the sea, a blue ache in the distant afternoon sun, always makes my eyes seem blue too'. But the sensual image is a powerful one. There is a strong sense, too, of the private consciousness actually altering the physical world in 'And the cloud, I can hear its lining slowly being ripped open, and wait . . . for the stitches of rain to fall apart.'

Another person objected to the incoherence of the thoughts. What was the connection between the various observations, between the wall, the sea, walking in step, having to rhyme, and writing itself? This is not an easy criticism to answer. The central idea, as the title suggests, is one of emergence, an intensely personal awareness of something about to happen, and this binds the first three paragraphs together. The next section, about rhythm and walking in step, loses that sense – which returns, in a baffling conjunction with the idea of rhythm, in the final two paragraphs.

On the plus side, however, its casual tone perfectly fits the elusive thought processes. She seems naturally to think in metaphor and images. At each new reading it keeps its spontaneity – it's a meditation, not an essay. An essay looks at a topic in a public way, and so has to be clearly understood. A meditation explores more private thoughts and feelings. In this sense it's 'writing from the inside'.

The term 'meditation' was first used in this way by Franz Kafka, in an early collection of one page or half page prose pieces to which he gave the general title *Meditations*. Nor was there anything new about a young writer producing brief sketches of this sort. Writers have always drafted short pieces which they can later incorporate, if they choose, into longer works. As a young man James Joyce coined the term 'epiphany' (literally, a 'showing forth'), for his descriptions of intense moments of a very personal nature – personal not in the common sense of private and therefore embarrassing, but rather, dealing with the kind of experience unique to the closed world of the individual. Joyce used several of these later in *A Portrait of the Artist as a Young Man*. There is a famous one when the young hero, based on Joyce himself, sees a young girl on the seashore whom he describes in an intense and poetic way in terms of a swan. Kafka, however, published his *Meditations* to be read on their own. Like Joyce (and both of them introduced this essentially modern element into literature) Kafka was concerned with the sometimes oppressive quality of the individual's private experience. For Kafka at least, it could produce an almost imprisoning sense of anxiety, something which later twentieth century writing is full of. Kafka have titles like 'The Street Window', 'Passers-by', 'On a Tram', even 'The Wish to be a Red Indian'.

Inside somebody else's world

If your own private world doesn't seem to offer the right scope, try somebody else's. This next piece shows yet another interpretation, entering the fictional private world of a real public figure. You may be able to guess for yourself which prominent politician the student who wrote this had in mind.

'An eastern story'

I live in a big house in a part of the world called The East. I am a child. People say that I am a man. I think it's the same thing. I am a man-child.

I am excited. I have been given a whole new toy-set. There are no pieces missing. I open it in the middle of the nursery. Millions of statuettes surround me. They are pawns I can play with. I set them all up.

I have been told I have strong and piercing eyes. These eyes do not like what they see. I kick out at a row of soldiers. They spray out from under my feet and lie scattered, broken. I shall bestow my favours on this statue, and this one. They are my generals, my spokesmen.

I am the Lord.

Lord? Don't say the word aloud. There was a rich man-child living in this house before me. People called him The Prince. He used to play, the same game. He used to call himself 'Lord'. And one day he fell down and hurt himself so badly that he has to beg for help now. His money is of no more use to him.

But I am clever. I will not make the same mistake. I will assume a guise. The robe of a priest. A long and flowing beard.

I am safe now. My mantle of religion is protective. It gives me strength and confidence. Walking back to the middle of the room, I kick some more statues. They fall and be still. That is good. I am in full control. The remaining toys shall form a tight circle around me.

I am invincible.

I can do anything.

And the neighbours shake their fists at me from the other side of the fence. I am too clever for you. You cannot pin anything onto me.

I continue playing with my toys. I knock them over, one by one.

The days pass.

There are few left standing now. I will set them all up again. I try. They fall. I try again. And again. It was a game then. Now, it has become an obsession.

In quiet desperation I try and make my toys stand. My

desperation turns to fear. I panic. I rush out of the nursery and hear my voice echo down the corridors . . . Nanny . . . Nanny . . . help me.

I run, I slip, I fall. My beard falls off, my holy garments are torn. There is no one to save me. I have to help myself.

For people call me the man-child.

While it has many of the qualities of any insecure megalomaniac, the specific character the student is entering into is the Ayatollah Khomeini. Obviously, much of the grotesque effect comes from placing him in a nursery lining up his toy soldiers, so that there is something pleasantly chilling about 'I rush out of the nursery and hear my voice echo down the corridors.' How cut off from reality *is* this hugely powerful character?

Now we are almost back where we were at the end of 'Finding a voice', with the private world of a created character, in a monologue. But there is a slight difference: whereas a monologue generally is concerned with a character and his ideas about things, a meditation is more about feelings, about a very private sort of world. And what we have with 'An eastern story' is not a realistic portrait of the Ayatollah, but a way in to his private world . . . his world from the inside.

It may be that you have found one of these kinds of writing more interesting than the others, and will try one yourself. Private images, rather than public ideas, are the key.

Finally, a look at two short meditations by Franz Kafka.

'Passers-by'

When you go walking by night up a street and a man, visible a long way off – for the street mounts uphill and there is a full moon – comes running towards you, well, you don't catch hold of him, not even if he is a feeble and ragged creature, not even if someone chases yelling at his heels, but you let him run on.

For it is night, and you can't help it if the street goes uphill before you in the moonlight, and besides, these two have maybe started that chase to amuse themselves, or perhaps they are both chasing a third, perhaps the first is an innocent man and the second wants to murder him and you would become an accessory, perhaps they don't know anything about each other and are merely running separately home to bed, perhaps they are night birds, perhaps the first man is armed.

> And anyhow, haven't you a right to be tired, haven't you been drinking a lot of wine? You're thankful that the second man is now long out of sight.

Here is that sense of anxiety, of indecision, I mentioned earlier. But what is extraordinary about it is the uncertainty of the 'context' of the piece. It begins apparently as a general consideration of what you do when somebody tears past you in the street at night, then it slides into nervous internal speculations about what these two 'imaginary' people were in fact up to, as the speaker defensively answers an imaginary charge of inaction, and finishes with a vivid, alarming sense of the present: 'You're thankful that the second man is now long out of sight.' A generalised worry becomes, in three short paragraphs, an extremely unsettling specific event. Kafka pulls off this trick again, even more deftly, in this last one. A single sentence takes us in a long breath through the development of a fantasy, the yearning for release in speed and motion. Release from what, isn't specified; but the sense of it is powerful in the images.

> 'The Wish to be a Red Indian'
>
> If one were only an Indian, instantly alert, and on a racing horse, leaning against the wind, kept on quivering jerkily over the quivering ground, until one shed one's spurs, for there needed no spurs, threw away the reins, for there needed no reins, and hardly saw that the land before one was smoothly shorn heath when horse's neck and head would be already gone.

9 *Making it real*

'Realism' in fiction can mean a number of different things. It can refer for example to a kind of writing where the visible world – how people dress, what they eat, how they speak and function in society – is made real in front of us, either by description or, just as important, by dialogue. The great nineteenth century realist writers such as Dickens and George Eliot, Balzac and Zola and Tolstoy, construct a fully realised and tangible world in their novels.

On the other hand, in some realistic writing almost nothing visible or physical is described, the sense of the story being 'real' coming instead from what people say, and how they say it, in flat, ordinary sentences, just as they do (supposedly) in the real world. So 'real' here means also 'everyday', the opposite of 'literary', free of stylistic tricks and cleverness.

Or again, sometimes people use it to mean gritty or depressing, as in 'a grimly realistic account of life in a Glasgow slum'. But of course you can be grimly realistic when writing about a life of luxury in a Knightsbridge flat.

Very few novels or stories written in the last couple of centuries aren't 'realist' in some way at least, if only in their subject matter. Unlike Homer, we tend not to write about gods intervening in human affairs, or men grappling with one-eyed monsters, or women turning sailors into swine. Unlike Shakespeare, we don't write about princes prompted to murder by ghosts, or wizards stage-managing shipwrecks. Characters in modern literature don't speak in poetry to each other, but in a way that more closely resembles the way people speak to each other in the real world. We can say, in fact, that realism mirrors the surface of everyday life. But there are different kinds of everyday life, and there are different kinds of mirror. So we end up with not one 'realism', but several.

Documentary realism

The nineteenth-century realist writer Balzac prided himself on being 'the secretary of French society'. That is, he saw himself as the chronicler of how people lived and how they operated in the world. He wrote about the stuff of everyday life – marriage, power, business, families, the Church. His novels, and those of the other nineteenth-century novelists, show us the world as it is lived, and subject it to a moral analysis in the process. Trollope, writing in the same period, even called one of his novels *The Way We Live Now*.

Here, for example, is Mr Bulstrode, the hypocritical banker in George Eliot's huge novel of provincial life, *Middlemarch*:

> Mr Bulstrode's power was not due simply to his being a country banker, who knew the financial secrets of most traders in the town and could touch the springs of their credit; it was fortified by a beneficence that was at once ready and severe – ready to confer obligations, and severe in watching the result. He had gathered, as an industrious man always at his post, a chief share in administering the town charities, and his private charities were both minute and abundant. He would take a great deal of pains about apprenticing Tegg the shoemaker's son, and he would watch over Tegg's churchgoing; he would defend Mrs Strype the washerwoman against Stubb's unjust exaction on the score of her drying-ground, and he would himself scrutinize a calumny against Mrs Strype. His private minor loans were numerous, but he would enquire strictly into the circumstances both before and after. In this way a man gathers a domain in his neighbours' hope and fear as well as gratitude; and power, when once it has got into that subtle region, propagates itself, spreading out of all proportion to its external means.

What makes Bulstrode 'real' is George Eliot's minute description of how he seeks and manipulates power – not in a crude and obvious way, but a subtle and painstaking one, for whom charitable works are a means of extending personal influence and control. There's something compulsive about his scrupulous pursuit, and this marks him out as perhaps not an evil man but certainly a dangerous one.

George Eliot shows us Bulstrode compulsively seeking control in numerous concrete incidents, as well as in the generalised description here of the Teggs and Mrs Strypes. Bulstrode would be a recognisable figure at almost any period in history, but he is also a uniquely nineteenth century mix of philanthropy, self-righteousness and obsessive control. In this passage George Eliot is the secretary of society reporting back to contemporary readers.

Few novelists now would care to be described as secretaries of their society. It is more likely they would talk in terms of seeking a more poetic or psychological or metaphysical truth. The focus has narrowed, and novelists tend to explore more provisional or partial visions, or look at the world more obliquely than Dickens or George Eliot did. The inner world has become more interesting than the outer one, so the task of documenting the way we live now has fallen in some ways to feature writers and journalists, whose writings continue the realist novel's fascination with how the observable world works – the way people talk, how they earn and spend their money, what they love and fear.

The American writer Tom Wolfe, in his excellent book *The New Journalism*, points out that good journalism and realist fiction share a number of techniques. For example:

a) Telling a story in scenes rather than via the author's narrative (in other words, showing not telling).

b) Relying heavily on dialogue rather than description, so that scenes unfold in front of the reader as in a play, rather than the reader being told about them.

c) Using physical detail to give a clear sense of the 'status life' of each character – meaning broadly who they are or would like to be in the world (see p. 61).

Wolfe accuses modern novelists of having retreated from realism into an obsession with the inner world or with the business of writing itself. In its crudest form, this is the novel about a novelist writing a novel . . . but it is also quite common for a novelist these days to assert that his novel 'is really about writing.' While for some the interest in what fiction is has proved a fruitful literary path – in Umberto Eco's *The Name of the Rose*, for example – for Wolfe this approach to fiction amounts to an abnegation of responsibility. Where are our chroniclers of the age, our Dickens, our Tolstoys, our Zolas? Wolfe's own journalism – his crackling accounts of America on LSD (*The Electric Kool-Aid Acid Test*) or the

United States space programme (*The Right Stuff*), for example – headed in this direction, but in the end he decided to have a go himself at the Dickensian novel of the 1980's.

The result was *The Bonfire of the Vanities*, in which the complacent life of a white Wall Street yuppie is shattered when his car knocks down a black youth in the Bronx. In the political and media circus which blows up around the case, Wolfe paints a detailed and scathing picture of the opportunism and hypocrisy of American society.

What makes the book of interest here is that it self-consciously observes all the rules laid down for the novel of documentary realism: lots of dialogue, lots of scene-by-scene construction and not much narration, and plenty of status-life detailed observation – of Park Avenue apartments, grimy Bronx courthouses, society dinner parties.

But it's also a reminder that obeying the rules of realism isn't enough. The fact is, the characters are stereotypes, there to represent particular social groups: the corrupt black politician, the seedy journalist, the snobbish wife of the financier. They're realistically portrayed, but they're not real, because they're not complex or surprising in the way characters in say, George Eliot's novels are.

Take this account of the main character, Sherman McCoy, walking his daughter Campbell to the school bus stop:

> Several little girls in burgundy jumpers, and their parents or nannies were assembled at the Taliaferro bus stop, on the other side of Park Avenue. As soon as Campbell saw them, she tried to remove her hand from Sherman's. She had reached that age. But he wouldn't let her. He held her hand tightly and led her across the street. He was her protector. He glowered at a taxi as it came to a noisy stop at the light. He would gladly throw himself in front of it, if that was what it would take to save Campbell's life. As they crossed Park Avenue, he had a mental picture of what an ideal pair they made. Campbell, the perfect angel in a private-school uniform; himself, with his noble head, his Yale chin, his big frame, and his $1,800 British suit, the angel's father, a man of parts; he visualized the admiring stares, the envious stares, of the drivers, the pedestrians, of one and all.

We get the picture, certainly, but it's no more than a picture of a rich man smugly showing off himself and his daughter. It's like a picture in an advertisement, designed to be instantly recognisable. And so it is, but what is instantly recognisable doesn't stay interesting for very long. Compare George Eliot's account of another powerful financier, Mr Bulstrode. Whereas Wolfe gives us the fact of self-satisfaction, Eliot gives us an insight into the secret workings of the springs of power.

Wolfe's 'documentary realism' is what most people would understand by the term realism. It's a style we're all familiar with, it's not tricksy or experimental. But it is a style nevertheless, with its own characteristics. And given that it is a style, it follows that there should be variations on that style. Here are two such variations.

Dirty realism

American literature has always had running through it a vein of bleak despair. It's the emptiness felt by the losers in the competitive dream, the drifters keeping desperation at bay in the stories of Hemingway, the plays of Sam Shepard, the songs of Bruce Springsteen, and countless Hollywood road movies.

Out of this vein in recent years has come a fiction to which has been given the name 'dirty realism'. It is a fiction peopled with characters from the underside of American life: mechanics, waitresses, truck drivers, cashiers, secretaries, petty thieves. The style is stripped down, flat, unemotional. The 'real' in this sort of realism is opposed to 'literary' – no frills, no refinements. Here is everyday life, says the author, uneventful, lacking in purpose, where people don't get to say what they mean even if they could figure out what it is they mean. But underneath it, or in the silences between the words, there is love and sorrow and fear.

In Raymond Carver's *Boxes*, a man and his wife, Jill, are invited to lunch with his mother, a woman always moving house and edging towards a breakdown.

> She makes coffee while Jill clears the table. I rinse the cups. Then I pour coffee, and we step around a box marked 'Knickknacks' and take our cups into the living room.
>
> Larry Hadlock is at the side of the house. Traffic moves slowly on the street out in front, and the sun has started down

> over the trees. I can hear the commotion the mower makes. Some crows leave the phone line and settle on to the newly cut grass in the front yard.
>
> 'I'm going to miss you, honey,' my mother says. Then she says, 'I'll miss you, too, Jill. I'm going to miss both of you.'
>
> Jill sips from her coffee and nods. Then she says, 'I hope you have a safe trip back and find the place you're looking for at the end of the road.'
>
> 'When I get settled – and this is my last move, so help me – I hope you'll come and visit,' my mother says. She looks at me and waits to be reassured.
>
> 'We will,' I say. But even as I say it I know it isn't true. My life caved in on me down there, and I won't be going back.
>
> 'I wish you could have been happier here,' Jill says. 'I wish you'd been able to stick it out or something. You know what? Your son is worried sick about you.'
>
> 'Jill,' I say. But she gives her head a little shake and goes on. 'Sometimes he can't sleep over it. He wakes up sometimes in the night and says, "I can't sleep. I'm thinking about my mother." There,' she says and looks at me. 'I've said it. But it was on my mind.'
>
> 'How do you think I must feel?' my mother says. Then she says, 'Other women my age can be happy. Why can't I be like other women? All I want is a house and a town to live in that will make me happy. That isn't a crime, is it? I hope not. I hope I'm not asking too much out of life.' She puts her cup on the floor next to her chair and waits for Jill to tell her she isn't asking for too much. But Jill doesn't say anything, and in a minute my mother begins to outline her plans to be happy.

There is a steady current of despair in this passage, against which struggle contradictory emotions of concern for the mother and anger at the consequences of her bizarre behaviour. The source of the despair is that it is now too late. His mother cannot be helped, but cannot be left to disintegrate. So where does the emotion come from in the writing?

Mechanical actions are described in a flat, mechanical way. 'She makes coffee while Jill cleans the table. I rinse the cups. Then I pour coffee, and we step around a box marked 'Knicknacks' and take our cups into the living room.' These are the small motions of everyday life, the necessary anchoring points in this unhappy (though superficially cheerful) world. They are a way of letting the moments pass by without pain. That is why we are told about them. It is the emotional weight they carry that makes them important. There is a wealth of emotional weight, too, in the 'Knickknacks' box. The word hints at a lifetime accumulating sad bits of junk which have to be packed up with every move.

And what of the flat description of the view outside: 'Traffic moves slowly on the street out in front . . . ' Does it matter that the crows have left the phone line? No, but it matters that the narrator is staring out of the window, flatly registering the details of daily existence. There's just the faintest hint of melancholy in the movement of the sun behind the trees. In every other respect, emotion is being squeezed out (which means it's there somewhere) rather than pumped up.

The dialogue is in a similar vein. When Jill says, 'I hope you have a safe trip back and find the place you're looking for at the end of the road,' in the polite, conventional sentiment ('have a safe trip') there is not only concern but also a feeling that the endless quest, ('the place you're looking for') is a futile one. Jill's outburst about her husband's waking in the night is the only piece of dialogue that has any urgency and directness. While her husband remains silent, his mother's response, like a frightened rabbit's, blocks out this revelation – of her son's anguish, of her part in it, and of the strain it is evidently bringing to the couple's relationship. Her apparently naive questioning as to why she can't be happy ('Why can't I be like other women?') tells us volumes about the depth of her self-delusion. She waits for Jill to reply, but Jill doesn't say anything. What is there to say?

In the fiction of the 'dirty realists' (writers such as Raymond Carver, Richard Ford and Frederick Barthelme), the stories – and this style is better suited to the short story than the novel – catch the characters just when their luck is about to run out, when love or death expose for a moment the vulnerability, the bleakness of their everyday lives. But the writing stays always on this flat, controlled level. In Richard Ford's *Rock Springs*, a couple break down in their car somewhere in the middle of Wyoming . . . he goes for help to a trailer home . . . they get a ride to a motel, exhausted and hungry . . . she decides she's had enough, she's leaving him. What will he do? Survive, somehow.

The irony is that although this bare-bones kind of writing gets its effect of being 'real' by stripping everything down to the minimum, this technique is just as literary, that is to say worked on and 'artificial,' as any other kind of writing. Raymond Carver quotes a story by Isaac Babel: 'No iron can pierce the heart with such force as a full stop put just at the right place.' The literary skill of someone like Carver lies in knowing exactly what to strip away and what to leave in. His story *Intimacy*, for example, consists almost entirely of angry words spoken by a woman to her ex-husband. Her stream of abuse is banal and clichéd: 'I've really had a bellyful of it, buster! Who asked you here today, anyway? I sure as hell didn't,' and so on. What gives the story its power is the continued silence with which the man listens to all this (apart from the odd murmur of assent), and a single action: 'Then here's the thing I do next. I get down on my knees, a big guy like me, and I take the hem of her dress. What am I doing on the floor? I wish I could say. But I know it's where I ought to be, and I'm there on my knees holding the hem of her dress.' He says nothing and does nothing else. And in this way a realisation creeps up on us of the pain and longing that lie buried beneath her words, and his silence.

This style also does something else. It creates tension. What's really going on here? It gives the reader something to do. Carver knew this of course: 'There has to be tension,' he wrote, 'a sense that something is imminent, that certain things are in relentless motion, or else, most often, there won't simply be a story. What creates tension in a piece of fiction is partly the way the concrete words are linked together to make up the visible action of the story. But it's also the things that are left out, that are implied, the landscape just under the smooth (but sometimes broken and unsettled) surface of things.'

Magic realism

What kind of realism is it when people float up into the sky, or fall from it without hurting themselves, or turn into strange beasts? It sounds less like realism than fantasy, something from The Arabian Nights or a computer game. But it would be wholly misleading to describe as fantasy such works as *Midnight's Children* by Salman Rushdie, or The *Tin Drum* by Gunter Grass, or *One Hundred Years of Solitude* by Gabriel Garcia Marquez. And yet such strange events and transformations take place in these books, often described as 'magic realist' novels.

In this passage from *Midnight's Children*, the people of India are counting the seconds to Independence, to be declared at midnight.

On the stroke of the hour will also be born the narrator of the novel, a boy with magical powers of understanding and communication.

> The monster in the streets has begun to roar, while in Delhi a wiry man is saying, ' . . . At the stroke of the midnight hour, while the world sleeps, India awakens to life and freedom . . . ' And beneath the roar of the monster there are two more yells, cries, bellows, the howls of children arriving in the world, their unavailing protests mingling with the din of independence which hangs saffron-and-green in the night sky – 'A moment comes, which comes but rarely in history, when we step out from the old to the new; when an age ends; and when the soul of a nation long suppressed finds utterance . . . ' while in a room with a saffron-and-green carpet Ahmed Sinai is still clutching a chair when Dr Narlikar enters to inform: 'On the stroke of midnight, Sinai brother, your Begum Sahiba gave birth to a large, healthy child: a son!' Now my father began to think about me (not knowing . . .); with the image of my face filling his thoughts he forgot about the chair; possessed by the love of me (even though . . .), filled with it from top of head to fingertips, he let the chair fall.
>
> Yes, it was my fault (despite everything) . . . it was the power of my face, mine and nobody else's, which caused Ahmed Sinai's hands to release the chair; which caused the chair to drop, accelerating at thirty-two feet per second, and as Jawaharlal Nehru told the Assembly Hall, 'We end today a period of ill-fortune,' as conch-shells blared out the news of freedom, it was on my account that my father cried out too, because the falling chair shattered his toe.

There is both magic and realism here: magic in the very narration of the story by the about-to-be-born infant (who will discover he shares telepathic powers with the other children born at at the same moment); and realism in both the historical event and the deliberately banal, everyday details of the birth – culminating in the clumsy farce of the dropped chair . . . which in turn proves to have bizarre and far-reaching consequences.

The point about magic realism is that the realism is quite as important as the magic. People remember the magic things because they're more unusual, but they take place in a world which is extremely real in the everyday sense. It's the curious relationship between the two, the describing of the extraordinary as if it were the same as the ordinary, that gives magic realism its unique effect. The Nazi Germany of *The Tin Drum*, observed by a small boy who never grows up, or the India of *Midnight's Children* are powerfully real places, shaped by politics and money and ideology.

So why should a writer choose to write in a 'magic realist' style? As usual, the reasons vary. In the landmark novel of magic realism, *One Hundred Years of Solitude*, Gabriel Garcia Marquez tells the story of Macondo, an imaginary Latin American village, over a century of stasis and change. A sense of the marvellous runs deep in the village imagination, and Marquez constructs a world where it is unsurprising that a beautiful girl should be assumed into heaven, but where the arrival of the first locomotive causes wonder and popular panic. Marquez' magical realism draws on the tradition of village storytelling to tell the story of the village itself, but uses the sophisticated realist style of the modern novel in the process. It's a long and circular tale, and while the march of South American politics occasionally impinges, the book reveals the history of the village, as imagined by its inhabitants, and realistically told, to be quite sufficiently rich in drama and fantastic happenings for any reader.

The central magical device of *Midnight's Children*, the extraordinary powers of the narrator – helps Rushdie to tell the story of India since that dramatic moment as a fable full of miracles and witchery, and at the same time as a chronicle of the birth of a modern nation, a process of blunders, opportunism and shattered ideals. Wherever Indian history is being made, the narrator Saleem is miraculously there, observing and participating in the mess.

Finally, in the hands of someone like Kafka, who must be regarded as an ancestor if not the father of magic realism, this style can generate a peculiarly modern sense of personal alienation, an existential sense of being in disharmony with the world. In Kafka's bleak universe, the strange things that happen come not from fable but from the nightmares of the modern soul. In *The Trial*, for example, the hapless hero Joseph K. tries doggedly to discover the charges on which he is being prosecuted by some capricious bureaucracy. But of course he never understands because the 'charges' are merely part of a confused and inexplicable world. This is how his classic short story *Metamorphosis* begins:

> As Gregor Samsa awoke one morning from uneasy dreams he found himself transformed in his bed into a gigantic insect. He was lying on his hard, as it were armour-plated, back and when he lifted his head a little he could see his dome-like brown belly divided into stiff arched segments on top of which the bed-quilt could hardly keep in position and was about to slide off completely. His numerous legs, which were pitifully thin compared to the rest of his bulk, waved helplessly before his eyes.

This unwelcome transformation is not only realistically described – 'his dome-like brown belly divided into stiff arched segments . . . his numerous legs, which were pitifully thin compared to the rest of his bulk' – but is the only unusual feature of what is otherwise a quite normal situation. His parents are having breakfast, his boss calls wanting to know why he's late for work. The consequences of this change – anxiety, frustration, loneliness, rejection and finally despair – are described in matter-of-fact detail. This matter-of-fact nightmare, as it unfolds, tells us not simply what it is like to be a beetle, but what it is like to be human. And we feel that humanity when we enter Gregor's world – a world that is accurately described, recognisable, realistic.

10 'A proper story'

Student: Look, this is all very well, but I want to know how to write proper stories.

Writer: Sorry, 'how to write' isn't allowed –

Student: OK, 'about writing'

Writer: – and what are 'proper stories?'

Student: You know . . . Oh, I've read about monologues and dialogues and first and third person narrative, and meditations and epiphanies and God knows what, but what about stories, you know, with a beginning, a middle, and an end. Where something *happens* instead of just being . . . meditated upon.

Writer: Like you read in magazines and anthologies?

Student: Exactly.

Writer: And with a plot?

Student: Yes, yes, with a plot! So that at the end the reader shuts the book with a snap and a satisfied look on his face, and says '*That* was a good story!'

Writer: How about if he's smiling and shaking his head, or thinking again about what he's just read and not feeling sure about it, or staring ahead in horror at the blank wall in front of him?

Student: That'll do, too.

Writer: Because whereas a *novel* generally gives you the feeling of everything having been sorted out . . .

Student: When the hero's chased the heroine for 300 pages and finally they're getting married . . .

Writer: Right . . .

Student: When the heroine finally realises in the seventeenth chapter that she's no longer a girl, but a young woman now?

Writer: And –

Student: – and when the railway finally reaches the town and with it brings the end of an era and the lives of its inhabitants will never be the same again?

Writer: Quite. Whereas in a short story . . .

Student: In a short story we're not concerned with following people over a period of time and watching them changing, moving towards something. It's more like . . . like a stone being thrown into a pool and the reader being left at the end watching the ripples expand?

Writer: Well, yes . . .

Student: So it's more likely to be an incident than a series of events. A dramatic incident that tells you something. Teaches you about life . . . which a novel can't do because you get all bogged down in psychology and realism and meditations and stuff.

Writer: Er, now hold on . . .

Student: Yes, I get it. One incident – POW! Leave 'em reeling, thinking about things. OK, right. Gimme a pen.

Hand over the formula!

Well, some progress has been made in one area at least – the differentiation between a novel and a short story. Each is suited to different things. Whereas in a novel we generally find a whole landscape, hills, valleys, plains, mountains, with a range of emotions and ideas of differing degrees of intensity and importance, in a short story we generally find the writer dealing with one emotion, one incident, one climax, a central idea. If the novel gives us hills and valleys, the short story takes us to a peak, and leaves us there. So that when writing a short story, attempting to handle too much can be a danger. Edgar Allan Poe, one of the 'founders' of the short story form, laid down in 1842 that a short story should aim for 'a single effect', a 'unity of impression.' And while there are some short stories which aim for more than this, as a working rule it's still a good one. It wasn't long after this that a 'moment of crisis' was judged to be essential, in which that single effect could most powerfully manifest itself. This is rather more problematic. Many stories, certainly, deal with a moment of crisis in someone's life when, our student would be glad to see, they learn something about themselves or other people; but there are also many masters of the short story who have developed a low-key approach to the form, so that their stories are more like a glimpse or a snapshot of a situation, in which the characters' 'crisis' may be ill-defined and from which they may not learn anything at all.

The student's claim to have cracked the secret of short story writing is obviously suspect, as anybody's claim would be. There are no secrets to be cracked in writing, and the student has seized upon one kind of short story, that which deals with a single dramatic incident, and is carrying it off in triumph, having found the formula. The idea that any good short story can be written to a formula has to be rejected. It might have seemed sensible to start categorising different *kinds* of short story (the crime story, the love story, the sci-fi story, the western story, the horror story and so on), and seeing what possibilities each one offered. But that would lead us straight into formula: every crime story must have a body, a motive, a detective, a hitch in the detection process, etc. A formula is easy to follow, a good story is hard to write.

This is not to deny that hundreds of short stories are written specifically to a formula every month, and published. The staff of teenage and romance and sci-fi and horror and mystery magazines regularly turn out short stories in which the basic ingredients are endlessly rearranged to produce the stories their readers want. The fiction editor of True Teenage Romance (for example) might draw up a list along these lines:

1 Handsome doctor trying to get over beautiful wife's death in car accident.
2 Successful dancer discovers she has contracted crippling disease.
3 Exclusive Club Mediterranné type chalet village in Tenerife.
4 Bullying business-man husband of dancer in search of his run-away wife.
5 Telegram found lying on hotel bed, after fabulous day exploring local sights, beginning REGRET HUSBAND/WIFE/FRIEND KILLED IN PLANE CRASH STOP.

Five minutes' work to draw up the list, another three to decide the order in which they are to go, and then pass it on to a sub-editor to flesh it out.

A characteristic of the finished product is that there will be nothing original, nothing fresh, about the situations in the story or the way in which they are handled, nor will the characters be anything more than cardboard cutouts wheeled around the story to keep the plot running on its predictable course. Any reader worth writing for will be bored by such repetition of recognisable formulae. Life itself and the relationships between people do not follow such set patterns, (nor in this case could the initial situation be described as anything other than artificially 'glamorous'). So we will leave *categories* of short story alone, and assume that we can talk about 'the short story', where people and the situations in which they find themselves are recognised as being important.

The distinction should be made before we move on between formula writing (as above), and the conscious use of devices or situations which have been used before. There is no need to set a precedent every time you think of a plot. The so-called eternal triangle, where A loves B who loves C, who may well love A, is a situation rich in dramatic potential that writers have always exploited, and will continue to do so. It looks, as a matter of fact, as if our fictitious fiction editor is heading that way too. Obviously, the success of a story depends upon the way it is handled. The cynicism in the editor's approach of knocking together basic ingredients is guaranteed to keep the finished product well within the limits of the formula story.

A full stop, or a straggle of dots?

To return to our student: it is to be hoped that all that stuff about monologues and dialogues will be seen to have relevance to all creative writing, including proper stories. Short stories have to be well written like everything else, their form has to be thought about, their settings have to be quite familiar in some way to the writer, and all the rest of it. Most of the different aspects of writing so far discussed will come together in different ways in any short story. The finished product that the student is after is the putting together of all these things. So is there anything about the finished product which is different from other literary forms?

One – singleness of effect – has already been mentioned. It is also significant that the student puts his finger on the *structure* of the short story: 'with a beginning, a middle and an end.' His point is a fair one. He's had enough of sketches. It's true that in most short stories tangible events happen and are felt to be leading to some sort of conclusion, so that we always want to know what happens next, unlike in, say, a sketch where something is being thought about or described. As one respected practitioner of the short story, Somerset Maugham, said, 'I preferred to end my stories with a full stop rather than a straggle of dots.' That's the way he liked to write. In his short story 'The Outstation', an isolated colonial of the old school is joined at his remote post in the jungle by an 'upstart', a company worker from a different social class. The old colonial is so incensed by the new man's boorish behaviour and indifference to custom (both native and colonial) that he finally contrives to murder him. End of conflict, end of story. A dramatic incident from its cause to its conclusion. The book snaps shut, the customer is satisfied.

Clearly-drawn characters, a strong story line and a satisfying conclusion appeal to many writers and readers. Bill Naughton, one of Britain's most popular short story writers, locates his stories firmly in a well-defined social setting, usually the North of his early life, exploits his intimacy with local speech to give his stories vitality and a strong realistic feel, and generally builds his stories round one incident of a dramatic or humorous nature. In 'Seeing a Beauty Queen Home', a young man, who obviously fancies himself with women, escorts a girl back to her grandmother's house late at night. The girl pretends to her gran upstairs that she is alone, but the old lady soon comes down to see for herself. Quick as a flash, the young man hits upon the idea of pretending to be a neighbour's son who has of course grown up a bit since she last saw him. He exploits the old lady's failing eyesight and the dim light, and his quick-wittedness pulls him through the interrogation. When the couple are left alone, he turns to the girl in triumph. She responds however by kicking him out of the house, disgusted by his skill at impersonation which to her suggests long practice. The table turned on the crafty hero, the story ends.

Such stories are the literary equivalents of anecdotes, or yarns recounted in the pub, or well-told jokes that build up nicely and have a satisfying punch line. As with such jokes, tell the plot before the story is read and the enjoyment is ruined. It's a kind of story telling that hasn't changed much since Chaucer's day, and in fact the device of a false identity is one that Chaucer himself used frequently.

But even Chaucer didn't always end his stories off with a full stop and a sound punch line. Not every reader likes things so neatly sewn up. The ripples of such a story, to use the student's metaphor, don't continue to issue from its centre. And the ability to produce continuous ripples is one of the short story's potential strengths, and one which many of the great short story writers exploit. In other words, they end their stories with a straggle of dots . . .

The clearest example of this technique being consciously adopted comes from the 19th-century Russian, Chekhov (another founder of the form) in his story 'The Bet'. In the first published version of the story, Chekhov tells how a wealthy businessman and a young lawyer have a reckless bet of two million roubles over whether the lawyer can voluntarily remain in solitary confinement for fifteen years. The lawyer moves into a lodge in the banker's garden and reads all the books the banker supplies him with, covering all the fields of human knowledge, methodically at first, then increasingly indiscriminately. On the eve of the completion of the fifteen years, the banker, now virtually bankrupt, goes to the cell to kill his 'prisoner'. He finds him asleep and haggard looking, with a note on the table. The note reveals that during his fifteen terrible years alone and meditating he has come to despise the banker and his millions, and to prove it will leave his cell five hours before the allotted time. The banker, filled with amazement and self-contempt, returns to his room. The lawyer indeed escapes. Several years later, however, a party at the banker's house is interrupted when the lawyer bursts in, desperate for money. The banker, overcome by the shock of his return and his demand, shoots him dead.

The tale as it stands has 'a beginning, a middle and an end.' Events have reached a bloody but satisfactory resolution by the time we finish, on a full stop. But when Chekhov included it in his *Collected Works*, he cut the final part and ended the story with the escape of the prisoner. This (the version now found in anthologies) leaves us pondering the reasons behind the lawyer's act, and the possible spiritual, psychological consequences for the banker. Chekhov was surely right in making this alteration. The power of the story is increased by the unnerving sensation of the implications being far from exhausted, of the ripples continuing to spread from its centre.

And Chekhov in fact said 'I think when one has finished writing a short story one should delete the beginning and the end', a method which led John Galsworthy to remark of Chekhov's stories that they were 'all middle, like a tortoise.' As such, they are significant scenes in a process which has begun before the story opens, and is understood to continue after the story has ended. This is very different from 'teaching a lesson about life', a function which any writer assumes at his peril. If a reader is keen to learn any lessons about life from literature then the moralist novel writers of the nineteenth century might be more suitable. It is in fact a feature of the short story that it often cannot be described as 'moral'. Its concern is more frequently with atmosphere, or mystery, or a brief evocation of the dynamics of a relationship. It creates a temporary world, explores an idea, and then withdraws. It can make a point, rather than teach a lesson. It is less well suited to the writer with a message to preach, than it is to the writer who has what Keats calls 'negative capability', that is, 'when a man is capable of being in uncertainties, mysteries, doubts, without any irritable reaching after fact or reason.' It is not surprising that many great short stories do not teach a lesson so much as depict an enigma, as we shall see later in the chapter.

Twist my tail, 4C!!

There is another feature often associated with the short story which has become valued out of all proportion, and that is the surprise ending. I once had the painful experience of having a seasoned English teacher interrupt my lesson to decree that 'a good short story has a twist at the end! 'The Monkey's Paw', Mr Birkett! Twist my tail, 4C, twist my tail!' She left me with the class, who were looking mildly anxious as they became aware yet again of their own experience being contradicted by the authoritative voice of a teacher. *Must* all stories have a twist at the end? Of course some do, the most famous being those of the American O. Henry. With great skill and ingenuity he repeatedly leads the reader to expect something other than what he gets, through such characters as Jeff Peters his brilliant confidence trickster. But used without enormous skill, such a device can be a feeble trick, propping up a weak story or serving only to invalidate, rather than add to, what has gone before, like the sad refuge of so many children writers, 'And then I woke up and it had all been a dream.'

If it works well, and it's extremely hard to do, then not only is the sensation of our expectations being upset enormously pleasurable, but we are then forced to see the preceding events of the story in a new way. In Henry James' classic tale 'The Turn of the Screw', a governess in a country house describes the terrifying happenings there (she sees ghastly faces at the window, and figures in the grounds) which convince her that the spirits of two dead servants are attempting to gain possession of the two delightful little children of the house. We become hugely involved in her struggle to protect them, until in the final pages she confronts them with these apparitions in an attempt to 'exorcise' them – but the children claim to see nothing, and are so terrified, perhaps as a result of her tactics, that one is killed by the shock and the other falls into a fever. The ending is ambiguous: is it the governess who has been manipulated by the powers of evil rather than the children? The reader is left in a whirl reconsidering the complex chain of events in a new but still uncertain way. The mystery of differing personal interpretations of reality was something that fascinated James in much of his writing, and while 'The Turn of the Screw' is, yes, a 'horror' story, and a 'story with a twist at the end', it is also about people and the realities of living. The 'twist' is a part of that reality, that uncertainty, rather than something used merely for effect – though the effect is stunning.

'The grim phantasm, FEAR'

We can continue our analysis of the kinds of things short stories are built around, and at the same time have a further look at the story that attempts to unsettle the reader. It should be obvious why the short story is so well suited to dealing with the unknown. A good story of this kind relies less on the gruesome or the macabre than on suspense or uncertainty, and these are more easily sustained for a short time than over the hills and valleys of a novel. What frightens us is as much psychological as external: and if the main character is uncertain about what is really happening, whether it's behind the locked door or within his own mind, then the chances are the reader will be engrossed in fearful curiosity too. The 'Gothic' stories of Edgar Allan Poe are frequently built round the nervous, excitable sensibilities of their main characters, who infect the world of the story with their personalities, super-receptive to perceptions and imaginings of evil. Most of his characters are mildly deranged in some way, reclusive aristocrats, moody scholars of arcane lore – the ones played by Vincent Price in the Hollywood versions of *The Masque of the Red Death*, *Ligeia* and so on. One such is Roderick Usher, acutely aware that his mind is unbalanced, and that this makes him a prey to horrible imaginings:

> I dread the events of the future not in themselves, but in their results . . . I have, indeed, no abhorrence of danger, except in its absolute effect – in terror. In this unnerved – in this pitiable

> condition – I feel that the period will sooner or later arrive when I must abandon life and reason together, in some struggle with the grim phantasm, FEAR.

The trouble with this is that it's rather overdone, rather too 'Gothic'. With somebody so obviously nutty we tend to remain detached from what is happening inside his head. The same principle works better in a story previously quoted, Poe's 'The Tell-Tale Heart' (see p.82) where the narrator meticulously murders an old man, by whose eye he has become insanely fixated, and buries him under the floorboards. The police come, and the narrator becomes horrifiedly aware of the beating of the old man's heart beneath the floor. The sound grows until it threatens to deafen him, and he hysterically confesses to the deed, driven to wretched distraction by the way the detectives mockingly ignore the din in the room. The detectives, it becomes clear, have heard nothing. This almost comes as a surprise, so far have we entered into the murderer's mind.

Perhaps the best example of a sensation of fear being created psychologically rather than by spooky events is in Ambrose Bierce's story 'A Tough Tussle'. A confederate soldier is alone on guard in a moonlit forest. He knows that his enemies are somewhere in the vicinity preparing for an attack. He makes out in the shadows the shape of a dead Yankee soldier under the trees. He is tired and edgy, the light is uncertain. As the night draws on, he wonders if the Yankee is really dead . . . or hasn't he just moved a fraction? All his rational education tells him that dead men don't move. But the night is a long one. His defences crumble, and he panics. He ends up slashing frantically at the corpse, and in despair as he realises the madness of his action he kills himself. When the two mutilated bodies are found the next morning, the reaction of his commanding officer as he shakes his head at the carnage is that it must have been 'a tough tussle.'

The strength of this story is that it can't be shrugged off, can't be dismissed as referring to things which 'don't exist'. When we read a story about 'The Thing in the Loft', it isn't hard for us to reassure ourselves that, well, there aren't any Things in *our* loft. With Ambrose Bierce's story, no such easy way out is allowed. It may be true that we are unlikely to find ourselves on solitary watch over a body in a moonlit forest. Nonetheless, we have all experienced times when all our reason and knowledge have begun to crumble under the test of fear. What continues to disturb about Bierce's story is not only the macabre quality of the act itself, but the uneasy feeling of the flimsiness of rational defences.

Finally, as an example of a story which could not be categorised as a horror story but which is certainly powerful and unsettling, Hemingway's 'The Killers'. The plot is a model of simplicity. Two men come into an empty lunch bar somewhere in America. It emerges they are waiting for a man, a 'big Swede', to come in so that they can kill him. They wait but he does not come. They leave. Nick, a boy serving in the lunch bar, goes to find the Swede and tells him. The man shrugs it off, hopelessly. He remains lying on the bed with his face to the wall. The boy returns to the lunch bar: 'I can't stand to think about him waiting in the room and knowing he's going to get it. It's too damned awful.' 'Well', says the barman, 'you better not think about it.' But the fact is the boy is going to think about it, and so is the reader, and about the boy's fear.

Snapshots

For a short story to reverberate in the memory, it does not have to contain a dramatic or violent incident as these do. As haiku is to poetry, so the short story can be to fiction; a snapshot, a scene or two which suggests preceding and subsequent scenes. Whether it's in the creation of a particular atmosphere for instance, or giving us significant scenes in a relationship, the feeling can be created that we have merely had a glimpse of something that has already been, and will continue to be, in existence. Obviously the world of personal relationships is ideally suited to such an approach. The story 'Funeral' (examined in chapter 7) exploits this well. Hemingway's 'Hills Like White Elephants' (page 46) deals with a couple's half hour wait for a train connection on a deserted Spanish station. Their conversation, which gets nowhere and is 'about' nothing very much, forms the bulk of the story. She remarks that the hills look like white elephants, and is irritated by his lack of response. She says things are no fun any more, he says they will be after her 'awfully simple' operation. In the end, she assures him she 'feels fine.' End of story. By this time we have been made acutely aware of the despair and frustration and self-deception in the relationship, and continue to brood over it, so powerful is the atmosphere of the story created by the sterile conversation and the lethargy of the dusty station.

Another writer who gives us perfect photographs of a relationship is Katherine Mansfield. Her stories concern missed opportunities, tiny but disastrous misunderstandings between people, the touching impossible dreams of lonely individuals. This is taken from 'A Dill Pickle':

> And then, after six years, she saw him again. He was seated at one of those little bamboo tables decorated with a Japanese vase of paper daffodils. There was a tall plate of fruit in front of him, and very carefully, in a way she recognized immediately as his 'special' way, he was peeling an orange.
>
> He must have felt that shock of recognition in her for he looked up and met her eyes. Incredible! He didn't know her! She smiled; he frowned. She came towards him. He closed his eyes an instant, but opening them his face lit up as though he had struck a match in a dark room. He laid down the orange and pushed back his chair, and she took her little warm hand out of her muff and gave it to him.
>
> 'Vera!' he exclaimed. 'How strange. Really, for a moment I didn't know you. Won't you sit down? You've had lunch? Won't you have some coffee?'
>
> She hesitated, but of course she meant to.
>
> 'Yes I'd like some coffee.' And she sat down opposite him.
>
> 'You've changed. You've changed very much,' he said staring at her with that eager, lighted look. 'You look so well. I've never seen you look so well before.'
>
> 'Really?' She raised her veil and unbuttoned her high fur collar. 'I don't feel very well. I can't bear this weather, you know.'
>
> 'Ah, no. You hate the cold . . .'
>
> 'Loathe it.' She shuddered. 'And the worst of it is that the older one grows . . .'
>
> He interrupted her. 'Excuse me,' and tapped on the table for the waitress. 'Please bring some coffee and cream.' To her: 'You are sure you won't eat anything? Some fruit, perhaps. The fruit here is very good.'
>
> 'No, thanks. Nothing.'
>
> 'Then that's settled.' And smiling just a hint too broadly he took up the orange again. 'You were saying – the older one grows – '

As the story develops, we become aware that his careful solicitude for her, his nostalgic but carefully selected memories of their relationship, are simply aspects of his selfishness, his desire to have things just so, and that this selfishness is even more entrenched in him than when they were lovers. He is not a swine, she is not shattered by the meeting. We are just made to see with marvellous delicacy the ways they both handle the meeting – he nostalgic and therefore detached, she still in some ways caught up in the relationship. She slips off in the middle of one of his speeches when he is being dismissive about the past.

> She had gone. He sat there, thunder-struck, astounded beyond words . . . And then he asked the waitress for his bill.
>
> 'But the cream has not been touched,' he said. 'Please do not charge me for it.'

The story is not only about the meeting but about their whole past relationship, and how they have come to view it.

The 'what if' story

There are of course an infinite number of possible short stories, and little is to be gained from devising endless categories for them. But there is another kind of story which we have not yet looked at which we might learn something from. It is a form which has come to prominence in our own times and in some forms could even be termed 'experimental.' It is the kind of story which is based upon a single idea, frequently a fantastic one, and which simply develops that idea in a literary way. It is less concerned with a realistic portrayal of a situation than with saying 'What if . . .' and then taking it from there.

In H.G. Wells' story 'The Country of the Blind', a wanderer gets lost somewhere in the Andes and crosses into a completely unknown land where all the inhabitants are blind. Initially he is pleased with his apparent superiority; but as the story progresses he comes to feel more and more like a freak, an outsider. He is on the brink of succumbing to suggestions of having an operation on his eyes when he breaks away and escapes, over the mountains. The story is a powerful study of the pressures of conformity.

A more aesthetic, purely fantasy approach is taken by Jorge Luis Borges, whose stories spring from ideas such as an infinite library in which all the possible books in the world are stored, (including billions of volumes of meaninglessly scrambled letters, or books which differ only in a single letter from their neighbour), whose librarians have trudged its stairways for centuries trying to find the supposed book which will provide the key to the library's system. In 'The Circular Ruins' a man trains himself to dream over a long period of time, until he creates a dream child over whom he has control. 'In the dreamer's dream, the dreamed one awoke.' The dreamer loves and fears for the boy. One day the dreamer sees a fire raging:

> For a moment, he thought of taking refuge in the river, but then he knew that death was coming to crown his old age and absolve him of his labours. He walked into the shreds of flame. But they did not bite into his flesh, they caressed him and engulfed him without heat or combustion. With relief, with humiliation, with terror, he understood that he too was a mere appearance, dreamt by another.

Unsurprisingly, science fiction writers rely heavily on the one-idea, what-if story. One of the best is Ray Bradbury, if only because his stories do not rely on the props and paraphernalia of sci-fi, the gadgets and time-warps and androids and the rest of it. He gets hold of a good idea, works it out on the page, and is a good enough word-magician to sweep us along with him. His short story 'The Traveler' is built round the idea that his main character, a witch-girl called Cecy, can 'inhabit' anything and anyone she chooses. The story is really a vehicle for him to explore what this would feel like. And because it's beautifully and imaginatively written, it's very entertaining to read.

The clear incident, ended with a full stop; the straggle of dots that leaves the reader thinking; the twist in the tail; the story that unsettles; the snapshot story; the 'what-if' story . . . there are plenty more kinds, but we would need an encyclopaedia to cover them all. Many stories spread over several categories, as is always the way with writing and categories. I have tried to avoid the stock notions of the horror story, the love story, the crime story and so on, looking instead at what has provided the basis for some good short stories, the idea or situation from which they start and the way in which that is treated, in the hope that some knowledge of the variety of forms a short story can take will have been gained. Some of them may have given you the germs of ideas for stories of your own. Once you know the form a little you are better equipped to make it work for you.

IDEAS FOR WRITING

Look back into your own past. You will almost certainly have been involved in incidents which you have continued to brood over or tell other people about. Use one as the basis for a realistic short story.

Newspapers are full of small articles that briefly recount a dramatic or even sensational incident – a woman is found throwing £5 notes from a bridge; three people are found dead in a car having committed suicide in the belief that the end of the world was only hours away. (Both these are genuine). Collect a few, and build a short story around one of them, adding fictional characterisation, motivation and the events which led up to it.

Shakespeare regularly borrowed plots from minor, even trashy, writers of his day. It is still perfectly possible to find the germ of a good story in badly written magazine stories or anthologies – in fact seeing it done badly will help you towards seeing how it might be done well.

Two people work together in a shop. Their relationship is one of mutual irritation, developing into hatred. The silent warfare between them is conducted through the petty incidents and routines in the shop. One of them decides finally to crush or humiliate the other one with a carefully, laid plan. The plan, however, backfires.

A funeral. As the mourners stand around the grave, the reader hears the thoughts of some of them. At the reception, the will is read out. The family and friends exchange a few brief comments. Over the course of the story an uncertainty about how the person died emerges. Alternatively, the manner of his death which seems unproblematic to the reader through the story suddenly appears to be other than that towards the end.

A girl works late in an office. She is perfectly relaxed, has plenty of work to do and plenty of time in which to do it. As the night draws on, she becomes increasingly aware of small noises in the empty building and of trivial, inexplicable events – objects not where she thought she had left them, and so on. Gradually her own certainty about her reactions begins to crumble, until she does not know if it is she herself or something in the building which is the cause of her fear. This leads her to a violent, irrational act.

A mother and son meet for their monthly lunch in a restaurant chosen by the mother. For both of them this is a ritual which they would not or could not forego, though for different reasons. In the snapshot of this regularly occurring appointment, try to suggest the forces at work in this relationship.

You are accidentally granted some magical power – to know what people are going to say just before they say it, to remember exactly everything that happened one year ago, to be in two places at once. This gift, or curse, only lasts twenty-four hours. Build a short story around one of those powers or a similar idea.

A reading list of short story writers

If you want to read, as well as write some short stories, this is a brief reading list. Such a list cannot fail to be anything but personal and incomplete and is specifically designed to accompany this chapter. If it were much longer it would be unmanageable, so many accomplished short story writers do not appear.

Of the writers who tend to end their stories with a full stop, are: Somerset Maugham, who frequently uses exotic settings for dramatic and finely crafted stories; Stan Barstow, Bill Naughton and Alan Sillitoe, who write stories with a clear story line and strong characterisation, often against a Northern working class background; and Frank O'Connor, whose sad and comic stories about Ireland and childhood are a treat.

The twist in the tail is the speciality of the American O. Henry, but also of the English writer Saki, who has a fine eye for irony and elegant grimness, particularly in the world of children.

Of the writers of stories which unsettle, my favourites are Edgar Allan Poe, Nathaniel Hawthorne and Ambrose Bierce, all 19th-century(ish) Americans. They seem to unsettle you deeply, rather than nauseate you with gruesome detail or bore you with spooks.

Ian McEwan produces strong reactions of admiration or of loathing from many people, with his stories about sex and adolescence. I'm one of the admirers. Roald Dahl I find less unsettling than irritating, with his complicated stories of people being nasty to each other.

The best writers of the modern variety of short story, looser on narrative but tight on suggestion and implication, are in my opinion: Hemingway (very prolific – recommended are 'The Killers', 'Indian Camp', 'A Clean Well—lighted Place', 'Soldier's Home', 'The Short Happy Life of Francis Macomber', 'A Day's Wait'); Katherine Mansfield, who specialises in delicate analyses of people and relationships; D.H. Lawrence, whose stories are boldly written, varied tales of men and women, nature, sexuality; James Joyce, whose single collection *Dubliners* can be read again and again, so subtle, even enigmatic, are the stories in it; the stories of Albert Camus, who also wrote only one volume, *Exile and the Kingdom*, are philosophical in nature but written in a beautifully clear and simple style.

Finally, of the short story writers who write non-realistic fiction, Jorge Luis Borges stands in a class of his own with his exquisitely written tales of intellectual fantasy. Mention is also made in the chapter of Ray Bradbury, who can turn his hand to most things, including straight sci-fi.

11 *What is a poem?*

That may seem a silly question. Thousands of people today show they know the answer simply by writing poetry, even if they couldn't give, or wouldn't be interested in giving, a theoretical answer. I once heard an English poet describe how he took on the job of editing an anthology of contemporary unpublished poetry, for which he invited entries from anyone who wished to contribute no more than two poems. For the next few months he made daily trips to the local post office to collect numerous large red boxes into which the postmen had placed the day's flood of mail for him. Writing poetry comes naturally to many people, and is indeed synonymous for them with 'creative writing'. Nonetheless, there are perhaps an equally large number of potential writers who shy away from it, regarding poetry with anything from misty-eyed awe to butch contempt. To some it is the 'spontaneous overflow of powerful feeling'* or 'pure', undisciplined emotion, to others it is an impossibly complicated intellectual pursuit, to others it is soppy, to others mystical. (Poetry of course can be all these things, though it won't all necessarily be good poetry). Young children often pick up that it means freedom, experimentation, intensity, and write poetry with far more spontaneity and enthusiasm than their seniors, who begin to get suspicious of unfashionable emotions, or put off by old-fashioned language, or paralysed by their compulsorily developed awareness of rhyme schemes, assonance, dissonance, metres and all the rest of it.

There is no shortage of *definitions* of poetry, particularly from poets themselves. Matthew Arnold said 'Poetry is nothing less than the most perfect speech of man, that in which he comes nearest to being able to utter the truth.' The Romantic poet Coleridge said 'Poetry = the best words in the best order.' Boris Pasternak, rather more entertainingly, 'It is the crunch of jostling ice floes, it is two nightingales duelling'. It is nice to know that poets consider themselves to be engaged upon the noblest of human activity, but it is not much help to us. How are the

*Wordsworth's definition.

nightingales made to duel? What are the best words? Why can't this be done in prose, which seems so much more natural to us? I was once asked by a student in a creative writing group to define the differences between poetry and prose. Having promised an answer in a few days, I thought about the jostling ice floes, the best words and so on. Finally she got her answer: 'Poetry, unlike prose, is divided up into lines and arranged on a page.' This seemed to me to sum it up pretty well, but she was horrified. She pointed out that prose could then be turned into poetry merely by arranging the words into lines on a page. This was true, as long as she realised that it wouldn't, again, necessarily be good poetry.

For instance:

'The Slopes of Mount Terror'

We have heard of Cape Crozier
(The eastern extremity of Ross Island)
Discovered by Ross, and named
After the captain of the Terror.
It is here
With immense pressures and rending
The moving sheet of the Barrier
Piles itself against the mountain.

It is here, also, that the ice cliff
Which runs for hundreds of miles to the east,
With the barrier behind it, and the Ross sea
Beating into its crevasses and caves
Joins the Basalt precipice which bounds the Knoll . . .

It is the kind of place
Where giants have had a good time in their childhood
Playing with ice instead of mud.

from *The Worst Journey in the World*
by Apsley Cherry-Garrard.

These lines, with only one or two minor alterations, come from a journal of Antarctic exploration, and the result is not a marvellous, but not an awful, poem. The arrangement of the lines makes us read it in a particular way, bringing out certain rhythms and emphasising particular phrases which help to bring out the grandeur and power of the scenery. It seems that only travel books will allow that kind of poetry to be 'found' ready made in their pages. But here's some social comment:

'Philip looks in on Soho's Big Clean-up'

Prince Philip
Gave the royal seal of approval
To the West End's clean-up campaign today
When he went walkabout
In the streets of Soho

The Prince
Exchanged the state carriage
Of the Queen Mother's birthday celebrations
For a fifteen-minute stroll
Through the gaudy streets that used to be congested with litter.
There was a happy surprise
For many Soho shopkeepers
As the Prince passed their stores.

For a crowded and often
Unrespectable area there was a complete lack
Of ugly incidents.

In Leicester Square
One of the resident tramps
Was prevented from making a rush
To button-hole the Prince
By security men.

This is taken entirely, including the title, from the *Evening Standard.* *

Just the fact that it's been made into a poem, with a 'little incident' given the important place at the end, makes us approach it in a different way, and in this case detect a sarcasm that we can be sure wasn't there in the original.

This technique, of 'discovering' poems in unlikely pieces of prose, is called 'Found Poetry' and it's good fun to do. Quite logi-

* Thursday, 17th July, 1980

cally, it can be done the other way round too, turning poems into respectable pieces of prose. If the poem has a regular rhythm and easily noticeable rhyme ('This is the Night Mail crossing the border/Bringing the cheque and the postal order') then the prose version of it will sound completely unnatural. A piece of modern free verse, however, could be written as prose, as in this 'version' of Richard Aldington's 'Evening':

> 'The chimneys, rank on rank, cut the clear sky; the moon, with a rag of gauze about her loins, poses among them, an awkward Venus. And here am I, looking wantonly at her over the sink.'

Quite simply, however, it does better what it wants to do as a poem.

> The chimneys, rank on rank,
> Cut the clear sky;
> The moon,
> With a rag of gauze about her loins
> Poses among them, an awkward Venus –
> And here am I looking wantonly at her
> Over the sink.

The spacing just makes it easier to read, slows us down in the right way for the mood of the poem, particularly, making us pause before the last two lines, and separates out the 'ideas' for us. It gives them, however simply, a kind of *form*. That's a word we'll have to come back to in another chapter.

The poet and literary critic William Empson quotes a fragment of a Chinese translation:

> Swiftly the years, beyond recall
> Solemn the stillness of this spring morning.

The two statements confront us, the making of some significant relationship is up to us. We connect, probably, movement in the first line and stillness in the second (though of course we may not do so consciously). Similarly, the years of the first line, and the moment in the second, and so on. This only points to the fact that the reader is likely to know what poetry 'is', will know its unwritten 'conventions', but that fact is important to the writer. It gives an indication of how the simplest, most basic use of poetic form, that of writing two lines separately in sequence, affects the way we look at a piece of writing.

The conventions of poetry have changed over thousands of years. Before men could write, and this is still true in many non-literate societies, poems were committed to memory with some sections improvised, by professional bards and recited at important occasions. Unsurprisingly they had strong regular rhythms and repeated phrases, an aid to memory among other things. With the development of writing, the 'pattern' of poetry came to include the eye as well as the ear. The simplest nursery rhyme shares a common origin with a sonnet of Keats or Eliot's *Four Quartets*. But do they have anything in common *now*, which, to go back to our student's question, make them different from prose? We have arrived at an exasperatingly simple distinction that poetry is spaced in lines on a page, but we should now ask, to what end?

Neither a rabbit, nor a bolt of lightning

If there is any one idea which links almost every writer of almost every kind of poem, it is the idea that somehow poetry involves magic – not in its creation, but in its effect. I mean magic here in a sense squarely between the magic of the professional conjuror and the magic of the 'primitive'. Between, that is, what is completely explicable and what is completely inexplicable. The conjuror's audience knows that somewhere he is concealing a struggling rabbit before he materialises it with a flourish (though unless he's an idiot he won't reveal where). The primitive does not understand why certain things happen (lightning, let us say), and ascribes them to a magical force which is not given to him, and will never be given to him, to understand. A poem is neither a rabbit produced from a top hat, nor a divine bolt of lightning, though it has something in common with both. The poet uses everything at his disposal to create his own kind of magic. If there is no sense at all of the marvellous when we read a poem, then it is perhaps a bad poem – unless of course it is we who are bad readers. The poet uses his knowledge of language, its associations, forms, rhythms and so on to create his magic. But he is hardly like the conjuror who knows perfectly well how his trick works. The poet will, every time, have to rely on instinct to help him juggle all the elements of his poem successfully. (Nobody can give you instinct, but you can train it and guide it. Perhaps that's why you're reading this book).

After his poem is finished he may marvel almost as much as an enthusiastic reader, not (not always, anyway) because he is swollen with conceit, but because he really won't entirely understand the process in the way that the conjuror does. There is no point in looking at a poem, then, as if it were a series of tricks. But nor is it a total mystery. A good poem has something of both. Here it might be safe to quote a poet's definition which could be of some practical use to us. The American William Carlos Williams said simply 'A poem is a machine made out of words.' The point about a machine is that it has to be designed, worried over, and built; and when it is built, it appears, almost magically, to have a life of its own.

It's high time we had a look at a complete poem. Here is 'Terrace', by Sue Shrapnel, from *Hackney Writers' Workshop Vol. 3*

'Terrace'

At the front, the houses try to part from each other,
fence fights with hedge,
paint rivals paint.
Net curtains defend: the defenceless are suspect.
Wallflowers compete.

At the back, dustbins and children and cats
and washing-lines open us out.
Smiles cross through kitchen windows,
hands cross walls with sugar and tools.
Children dream in the yard as their parents row in the house;
a man mutters to the onions, wagging a finger;
a woman stands short of breath with pegs in her hand.
At night, someone with a skinful
kicks a bottle;
at dawn, a brick scrapes
as a lover uncovers a key.
At the back there are no secrets, but we all keep them.

At the front, everything is hidden, and talk is merciless.

If you like this, you may be led to wonder what makes it a good poem. Its main idea is really very simple, the contrast drawn is a straightforward one, the lives of the people concerned couldn't appear less unusual. The language isn't showy or elaborate. Yet personally I often find myself looking at terrace houses and thinking about that poem, and vice versa.

For one thing, it's a lovely relaxed view of backyard communities. Everything is clearly and perfectly observed:

> At the back, dustbins and children and cats . . .
> a woman stands short of breath with pegs in her hand

The details are right, and there's always a charm simply in that, in being taken so quickly and fully into the world of a poem. But as in a well-edited film, the details are helping suggest an idea:

> Smiles cross through kitchen windows
> hands cross walls with sugar and tools.

We're bound to respond to the image of hands crossing walls, particularly after we've been told how at the front, the houses try to part from each other. But it's only 'sugar and tools' that are being handed over, there's no need to be romantic about this down-to-earth communion. There *is* a feeling, though, a sense of marvel at the ordinary, of love even, for the familiar noises of the backyard, the bottle breaking, the brick grating. Then:

> At the back, there are no secrets, but we all keep them.
> At the front, everything is hidden, and talk is merciless.

Nowhere does the poem directly ask why, but the question, and an answer, is implicit in it. So we don't feel we are being preached at, but that an idea is being worked out in front of us. The idea isn't presented baldly to us at the beginning, it's stretching its limbs on the page. In that sense it's a performance – and here we might risk another definition, not anybody else's this time, that a poem is the performance of an idea. And you can't have one without the other.

I began with 'Terrace' because without being elaborate or complex, it does exemplify several things common to most good poems. A good use of images, first of all. An image is a word-picture, in this poem of a fairly straightforward kind: 'fence fights with hedge', 'Smiles cross through kitchen windows'. There's plenty to see and hear. It contains an idea, upon which the poem is built, the contrast between back and front. Her language is simple, but is used not only to sketch precise images, but also to pinpoint paradox:

> Net curtains defend: The defenceless are suspect . . .
> At the back, there are no secrets, but we all keep them.

Finally there is feeling, intensity, seriousness, sincerity, whatever we choose to call it. She cares about what she is writing without tipping her emotion all over us. So it's feeling with control.

We can perhaps draw up a list of the four things which we consider important in writing poetry:

> A poetic idea, on which the poem is built, the angle from which it approaches its subject matter.
>
> Imagery, which roots the ideas and emotions of the poem in the physical world.
>
> A sensitive use of language, that is, the feel for the right word, which can sometimes be the plainest one, at the right time.
>
> Feeling with control: feeling needs to come through if we are to respond to the poet-in-the-poem. (This is not to say that he has to be sincere all the time and say only what he thinks. He can play roles as much as he likes, so long as each one convinces us.) Feeling won't by itself sustain a poem. It needs to be drawn into the poem's whole.

The list is slightly absurd because any such list would be. No good poem was ever written to a recipe, and plenty of good poems could be found in which other things are more important. But it will do as a working rule.

12 *Just a few lines*

Wisely forgetting our poetic list for a while, we could think about beginning to write some poetry straight away. But there are few things more frustrating than the generous invitation to write a poem about anything. So this will have self-imposed restrictions in the hope of providing a simple framework and discipline. The form I want to begin by looking at is a traditional Japanese one known as haiku. The rules are strict. The aim is to present an image, evoke a mood, or make an observation – in three lines. What's more, the number of syllables per line is also controlled: five in the first, seven in the second, five in the third. This 'perfect' haiku is by a girl of 12.

	syllables
Running through the snow	5
Cold and numb gallops the horse	7
Challenging the train	5
	total 17

This 'imperfect' haiku is by the American poet Ezra Pound.*

'In a station of the Metro'

The apparition
Of these faces in the crowd;
Petals on a wet, black bough

It is 'imperfect' only in the sense that the last line contains seven rather than five syllables. But like the girl's above, it presents an image, or rather, two, which trigger off a kind of emotional response in us. In the girl's, it is perhaps a simple one of admiration for the

* Pound wrote the poem in two lines: but otherwise it follows the haiku format.

cold, numb horse, pitted against the train. In Pound's, the word 'apparition' gives the poem a dream-like quality, which is picked up again in the last line 'Petals on a wet, black bough' which suggests a special kind of sympathy with the anonymous faces on the platform.

Many haikus, including the two above, work in much the same way as a photograph, primarily on the visual level. And, like a photograph, they present an image in such a way and in such a relation to the other things in the poem (or photograph) that we 'read' the finished product as a whole. In this case, we see the faces in the metro and the petals together. Within the poem they are the same thing. Already we can see what can be done in three lines.

This is a famous haiku, also by Pound:

'Fan-Piece, for her Imperial Lord'

O fan of white silk
Clear as frost on the grass blade
You also are laid aside

We are probably struck by the beauty of the central image, but immediately we have to read it again. Whatever the poem is 'about', we can see, almost touch, the fan itself. The title helps us, but the word 'also' is interesting, too. It suggests a whole range of experience similar to, but outside, the one in the poem. It's happened before. The speaker, we guess, is a figure in some kind of court intrigue, whose identity isn't certain. There's plenty for the reader to 'do' here.

There's plenty for the writer to do with haikus, too. The aim is perfection of a sort, and that's always worth striving for. Any experience will do for your material – a view from a train, an action caught in snapshot, a mood, a comparison. But keep to the rules as a form of discipline, and keep revising and rejecting until you have the essence of what you want to do. Of course you may not know exactly what you want to do until you see it on the page in front of you. That's half the fun. The haikus that follow are by some of my students.

'Bank Holiday Heatwave'

Between the quick scoop
And the greedy lick, a sadness:
Warm vanilla on the knuckle

'Moments later'

Fingers sweat-cool, eyes
defreeze their ardour; already
sunlight trails on cold water

'Loneliness'

Thoughts clawing the night
for touch-familiar-warmth; but
only a firebreak in the east

'Hysteria'

Bewildering splits
and tricky little metal zips
revealing the unconscious

'Old pair of sandals'

My foot's curled imprint
Sleeps in the patient leather
Ready for my careless dash

Without the trappings

We can now go on to think of other ways of writing satisfying poems which don't take six weeks, and if we're lucky not even six minutes. One of the good things about a haiku is that it's so short there's no room for vagueness or waffle. It's got to be clear and sharp. 'Vagueness' is in fact something that has always been a problem with the writing of poetry. Poems can often look 'poetic' if they wrap themselves up in an artificial, or sentimental, or old-fashioned kind of language: but give them a push and the icing falls off to leave nothing very interesting underneath. Around the time of the First World War, a group of poets calling themselves 'Imagists' began to reject the kind of poetry which reflected and glorified the self of the writer, or which relied on elaborate poetic language to disguise the essential banality of the thoughts. They wanted poems to be 'hard', impersonal, relying heavily on precisely constructed images. Ezra Pound was one of the foremost

Imagist poets, and said, interestingly, 'Poetry must be as well written as prose' – by which he meant that it was no use dressing up stale ideas and sentiments in the outward forms of poetry if they would be exposed for what they were in plain prose. Richard Aldington's poem 'Evening', quoted in the previous chapter, is an 'Imagist' poem, and we've seen that it stands up pretty well to Pound's test. It isn't being propped up by anything.

This is one of their 'poems without the trappings':

'The Encounter'

All the while they were talking the new morality
Her eyes explored me.
And when I arose to go
Her fingers were like the tissue
Of a Japanese paper napkin

Ezra Pound

Even in these five lines we do in fact find our four elements: *imagery* and a *sensitive use of language* – the paper napkin image at the end most strikingly, but there's also a note of contempt in the phrase 'talking the new morality'; *poetic idea*, the idea upon which the poem is based, here the gap between the hot air being talked and the action going on silently; and *feeling with control*, in the ironic tone of voice used to make the point.

Of course we might complain that we've never actually *felt* a Japanese paper napkin, and that this delicate observation-making is a bit 'precious'. Doesn't the combination, though, of 'tissue', 'Japanese' and 'paper' *suggest* an extreme sensual lightness, even if we've never been near the thing itself? Some people at the time were quick to notice the dangers of this style, and a parody was written which poked fun at just this:

'Selected Bulbs from a Javan Pot'

Wondering how I would be able to pay my
laundress, I let my eyes fall and I saw the
smutty tamarinds I grow in my little window-box

The idle life of the literary dabbler is mocked in the mention of the laundress and the exotic flowers, but there's more to it than that. The writer of the parody has pushed the three line poem over from lightness to triviality. It doesn't work as a *poem* (deliberately) because the two images (laundress' bills, smutty tamarinds) don't 'charge' each other. There is nothing dynamic in the gap between them, they are not in any interesting relationship to each other. Unlike Pound's 'Encounter' where the talk and the touch are in a relationship of ironic contrast. Or the haiku 'Moments Later', where the bodily images (fingers, sweat, eyes) 'charge' the natural ones (sunlight, cold water) and vice versa.

Here's another example of an 'Imagist' poem:

'Oread'

Whirl up, sea –
Whirl your pointed pines
On our rocks
Hurl your green over us,
Cover us with your pools of fir

by H.D.

This will also help to introduce what is in many ways the staple of poetry: metaphor. Metaphor, any schoolteacher will tell you, is a way of comparing one thing with another without using 'like' or 'as'; and it's usually paired with simile, which is a comparison which *does* use 'like' or 'as'. But the comparison isn't always conscious in metaphor. There's nothing very sophisticated about metaphor, we use it all the time. Look at the following sentence: 'He came storming into the bar, a mountain of a man with a bull neck and cauliflower ears, shot a look at the barman and exploded with laughter.' A bit startling as a sentence, but each phrase is a perfectly ordinary expression. Each phrase is also metaphorical. The man is compared to a storm, a mountain, a bull, a cauliflower, a gun, a piece of dynamite – except that we don't really notice the comparison because the phrases are so common. We do notice it in metaphors in good poetry because they are fresh and original.

The poem above, 'Oread', is based on one metaphor, that of 'the-sea-as-pines'. There have been a million poems about the sea but this is new because the metaphor is new. Just as you can hardly speak without using some kind of metaphor, so a poet comes to write in metaphor almost as second nature:

The day *dispossessed* of light. At four o'clock
in the afternoon, a sulphurous, *manufactured*
twilight, *smudging* the scummed lake's far side
leant on the park

from *'October in Clowes Park'* by Tony Connor (with my italics)

A poem, then, particularly of the kind we are considering, can be built around a single metaphor*. The same is true of a simile. These next three, by students, are of the second kind.

'Marauder'

Invading my heart,
Like a cloud of jet-black ink
From a squid, is love

'Resurgence'

You jump in and out of my life
Like some bad-mannered
Out of time Jack-in-the-box.
Just when I have changed
Just when I need you least,
You come jumping back
With only a slight limp

'The Sip'

Like wine
I feel him in me
Warming the world
With his colour

This one, translated from a classical Indian language, uses two similes to make a relationship of contrast:

'What she said'

When my lover is by my side
I am happy
as a city

* See also Chapter 13, 'Ideas into Shape'.

in the rapture of a carnival,
and when he is gone
I grieve like a deserted house
of the wastelands
where the squirrel plays
in the front yard

Seeing double

In all creative writing, relationships between things (words, images, situations, events) are of overriding interest. We have seen relationships at work in the two-line fragment:

Swiftly the years, beyond recall
Solemn the stillness of this spring morning

They are there in Pound's 'Encounter', and absent in the parody, 'Selected Bulbs'. One of the most interesting relationships in writing is that of irony. It's not an easy word to define, but we recognise it when we see it, and in fact use it ourselves all the time. When a person sourly says 'Charming!', we know by their face that they mean quite the opposite, and we respond to the relationship between what they say and how they say it. That familiar kind of relationship is not, perhaps, incredibly fascinating (what I've just written is another kind of irony, that of understatement). We see this too in the comic-book slang as the flak-shredded fighter pilot staggers into the mess and says quietly, 'Spot of bother over the Channel . . . Jerry wanted a dust-up so I obliged . . . suppose I'll need a bit of sewing-up.' Again the effect is in a relationship, between the nature of the situation and what's said about it.

When someone speaks to us, we can see the expression on their face and react accordingly. When someone speaks in a deliberately deadpan way, we have to guess a little at how they want their words to be taken. And when a writer writes ironically, we are made to work a little harder than that. As soon as we grasp the writer's intentions, we feel we know something not immediately obvious in the statement.

'By Omission'

Time
For my black brother
Began with his slavery
Or so my history master said.

Les Skeates *(Hackney Writers' Workshop)*

We are immediately drawn into a conspiracy with the writer against the history master who makes this statement – the 'interesting relationship' being between the facts of black history and the assumptions behind the schoolmaster's remark. We are seeing double, through the eyes of the writer and of the speaker.

Talk about irony always runs the risk of being obvious because irony is such a common part of our speech. The schoolboy who wrote this poem didn't need to be told what irony was:

'Broadminded'

Some of my best friends are white boys.
When I meet 'em
I treat 'em
Almost as if they was people

Ray Durem

Nor do we as readers need to have it explained. Nonetheless, it isn't always easy to see how it works. Yet the process is essentially the same for this poem as it is for what is perhaps English Literature's most famous ironic sentence: 'It is a truth universally acknowledged that a single man in possession of a good fortune must be in want of a wife.' Universally acknowledged by whom, we wonder . . . and enter into a conspiracy with Jane Austen as she satirises the matchmaking mothers of the English upper classes. It is a conspiracy because it is a way of mocking someone without them knowing about it. The history master's statement, too, appears to be given absolutely 'straight'.

Irony clearly can't be confined either to poetry or to prose. But it should also be obvious that the ironic tone of voice is extremely well suited to the poem of a few lines, as we have seen above, and also in the student's poem below. In all three examples, thought processes are started and left for the reader to finish.

'Revelation'

Exhibitionist
I am:
baring my soul
to anyone who will tell me
it is still there.

Again, we are left thinking about the two apparently contradictory statements, and the relationship between them. D.H. Lawrence, too, was fond of the ironic, and here also very bitter, tone:

'The mosquito knows'

The mosquito knows full well, small as he is
he's a beast of prey.
But after all
he only takes his bellyful,
he doesn't put my blood in the bank.

One thing to notice about many of these poems is how much can be done with a title. 'Fan-Piece, for her Imperial Lord' puts the feelings of the poem into an elaborate context. 'Moments Later' immediately presupposes an event, the nature of which we must guess at from the poem itself. 'Broadminded' prepares us, quite deliberately, for something slightly different from what we get. A good title helps you create a context, or strike a tone of voice, which will lead the reader to expect something. It may not be quite what the reader expects, of course.

Writing poetry of this kind shouldn't be seen *only* as a stepping-stone to writing longer poems. Haiku, for example, is a form many Japanese poets spent years perfecting and polishing. The aim of such poems is generally to make a point, or an observation, and withdraw. As such they need a sense of economy and a lightness of touch. These are also, in fact, qualities which will prove valuable in attempting any longer work. In the writing of poems like these, you should be able to start developing a practical understanding of the relationship between images, the use of simile and metaphor, and the possibilities of irony, all of which are fundamental to any kind of creative writing. You should also have an early taste of what every writer, professional or amateur, needs: a finished product to show for your efforts.

IDEAS FOR WRITING

Keeping to the rules if you can, write one or more haikus on any topic, using this list of suggestions if you need to:

Peeling an orange
A passerby seen from your window
The rain in the street
A bird on the chimney
A moment of anger
Traffic jam
An animal moving

Write a poem of a few lines which uses a simile or a metaphor to give it form (see pages 142–152). Short love poems, or poems which express an intense emotion, are well suited to this.

Leave a short note for someone in the form of a poem giving what looks like an apology for something you've done. This could benefit from being ironic.

Use the following 'pattern' to write a short poem:

What I like about . . . is its . . .
What I hate about . . . is their . . .
What I like about . . . is her . . .

Write a poem describing the images you see as you drift off to sleep, or daydream.

Again using only images, write a short poem describing any of these:

Bank holiday on the beach
Winter evening
Memories of childhood
Household noises
Motorway service station
Private fears

13 *Ideas into shape*

Arranging your ideas

If we are agreed that the major characteristic of poetry is that it is arranged in lines on a page, we might also try and find out what kind of 'arranging' can be done and what effects it has. This chapter looks briefly at some of the different kinds of 'shape' or 'form' or 'structure' or 'pattern' a poem can have. The fact that words like 'shape' and 'pattern' are being used should reassure the reader that what follows is not a detailed, complex list of the different rules which apply when writing heroic couplets or quatrains, or whatever*. The simple fact is that poetry writing these days is not governed by rigid rules in the way that it was in, say, the 17th and 18th centuries. It is, nevertheless, important to consider what kind of 'shape' a poem is going to have, and how this might help you do what you want to do. After all, a poem is the performance of an idea, not just the statement of it.

The 'arrangements' which give a poem shape can be of many different kinds. There could be a rhyme at the end of each line, or every other line:

How fevered is the man who cannot look
Upon his mortal days with temperate blood,
Who vexes all the leaves of his life's book
And robs his fair name of its maidenhood.

These lines in fact not only rhyme alternately, but have a clear rhythm to them – there are five clear beats in each line:

How févered ís the mán who cánnot lóok
Upón his mórtal dáys with témperate blóod

* Those who are interested in the technicalities of poetry are recommended to try Robin Skelton's excellent book *Teach Yourself Poetry* which contains a fair amount of technical instruction.

So in these lines of John Keats', we derive a sense of shape from both rhyme and rhythm.

Or, there are sometimes whole lines or parts of lines repeated at a particular point in each verse in a refrain or chorus, as in this extract from a poem by a 14 year old, Sarah Gillam:

> I gave the letter to the old man's wife.
> I knew the problems would lie ahead.
> 'John fought hard', or so they told;
> The rain fell hard, the mines, the dead.
>
> I saw her cry, the old man's wife,
> I dried her eyes, pulled back her head,
> 'John died fighting', or so they told:
> The rain fell hard, the mines, the dead.

This kind of pattern is borrowed from the old ballad form, which was often sung, and therefore needed a regular rhythm. The choruses provide a pleasing bit of familiarity in each verse, and can serve to drive home the important images, in this case, of death and horror.

A pattern may be evident in the way the ideas of the poem are presented, so that the reader feels the thoughts and the actions following a pattern, as in this type of question and answer poem:

> 'O what do you here so late?' said the knight on the road,
> 'I'm going to meet my God' said the child as he stood,
> 'O how will you go by land?' said the knight on the road,
> 'With a strong staff in my hand,' said the child as he stood.

and so on. The boy is being tested by the knight (the devil disguised) and his questions become more and more menacing. So while there is repeated pattern, it also allows for development.

Or a poem may follow a pattern laid down by established rules. A sonnet, for instance, *has* to have fourteen lines, and these fourteen lines are themselves governed by rules about rhythm, length, and development of ideas. (An example is given on page 148).

Or, finally, it may only be from the development of the ideas and emotions that a sense of shape or structure emerges, in the way, for example, that the poem leads finally towards some kind of resolution. George Herbert, in 'The Collar', spends most of the poem grumbling and fretting about the priest's life he has to lead, but the poem finishes:

> But as I raved and grew more fierce and wild
>   At every word,
> Methought I heard one crying 'Child',
>   And I replied, 'My Lord'.

This is not to say that *every* poem has to have a noticeable shape or form. What a clear form can help to do is give a poem 'personality' – a word borrowed from the poet Robin Skelton, who gives a marvellously precise definition of what form is. Established forms, he says, tend 'to limit the personality of the poem, and therefore to strengthen and define it'. Personality in poems is linked with their pattern, their shape, their feel. The pattern of a poem, made up of its rhythms, its rhymes, its repetitions, its paradoxes, the arrangements of its ideas and so on, will make it crude, or subtle, or enchanting, or low-key, or monotonous, or whatever. All these things, together with the imagery and the tone of voice used, help to turn lines on a page into a 'performance'.

The external features of a poem (like rhythm and rhyme or the rules which it is following) frequently work together with the internal ones (the way in which the ideas are presented) to create the structure of a poem, each one strengthening the other. This is in a sense only an extension of the idea outlined in chapter 11 'What is a poem?', that two lines written one after the other are placed in some kind of relationship with each other.

For discussion purposes, the external and internal features of a poem will be looked at separately.

Rhyme and rhythm

The most obvious thing to say about rhyme is also the most important: don't let your need for a rhyme dictate what you want to say. You'll end up twisting the sense uncomfortably. (Rhyme used well has just the opposite effect: it gives a statement a feeling of ease and perfection.) Someone wanting to write a love poem, for instance, has to watch out they don't fall into the arms/charms, tears/fears, ruby lips/fingertips trap.

These days, rhyme is much less frequently used than it used to be. But it's worth noting that rhyme is very popular: two of

Britain's best-selling poets, John Betjeman and Pam Ayres, rely on it heavily. Greetings cards are nearly always rhymed and presumably give satisfaction because they are so. It's our need for pattern again, which comes out very strongly in song. Song always has a musical pattern (that's after all what music is), and nearly always a verbal pattern. One effect of rhyme can be to give a satisfying sense of neatness, of finality:

Sexual intercourse began
In nineteen sixty three
(Which was rather late for me)
Between the time of the Chatterley ban
And the Beatles' first LP

from 'Annus Mirabilis' by Philip Larkin

Or in the hands of someone like W.B. Yeats, who never lost his hold on strong, well-formed verse, strongly rhymed and rhythmed, it contributes to the effect of magical spell, of unassailable wisdom:

Many times man lives and dies
Between his two eternities,
That of race and that of soul,
And ancient Ireland knew it all.
Whether man die in his bed
Or the rifle knocks him dead,
A brief parting from those dear
Is the worst man has to fear.

Poetic ideas

As suggested earlier, a poem's shape can come as much from inside as from outside, in the way that the ideas and emotions are presented. It can in fact come entirely from what is referred to in 'What is a poem?' as a 'poetic idea'. A 'poetic idea' might be defined as a 'slant', an 'angle', a 'device' around which a poem can be built. In 'Terrace' it was the contrast between what happens at the front and what happens at the back of people's houses. In the following (student's) poem, the angle, the ideas which gives the poem its shape, is the similarity and contrast between love in the world of advertisements and love in real life.

'Light up'

Our heads almost touching
Our hands the other's cupping
We strike a match
                    And light up,
The glowing orange warmth spreads
Radiates and sparkles from your face
And in the loveliness
                    I breathe.
Surely smoothness has never been so
                    satisfying.
But
Moments that happiness blends
Moments and moods
          That set the made for each other
                              trend
The Surgeon General advises
And statutorily Warns –
               As butts,
               Must soon be tossed away

The idea is taken further to make the comparison between smoking and love: the 'butts/must soon be tossed away.' What makes the poem go on surviving re-readings is the deftness with which he mixes the false sincerity of the advertising world, the ambivalence of the spark of tenderness and the lighting of a cigarette, the nasty after-effects of both, and the play with the stale clichés of advertising language:

Moments and moods
          That set the made for each other
                              trend

The notion of a poetic idea is nothing particularly new. Love, for example, has always been elaborately, sarcastically and joyfully compared with other things, from the pair of compasses in John Donne's seventeenth century poem, to the twentieth-century cigarette advertisement, quoted here. Just as poets have always adapted ideas and the form with which to express them from previous poems, so it would be useful to you to look out in the poems you read for the governing idea which a poem is structured around and how it is used. Time spent experimenting with old forms is often time well spent.

Bob Dylan's great song 'A Hard Rain's A-gonna Fall', uses a question-answer ballad form, most well-known in the traditional 'Lord Randal'. The poem begins:

O Where have you been, Lord Randal my son?
O Where have you been, my handsome young man?

and these lines are used at the beginning of each verse, to which the son gives enigmatic and increasingly ominous replies. Finally it emerges that his lover has poisoned him. Dylan's song keeps the questions, slightly adapted, at the beginning of each verse, to which the replies are all descriptive of a horrifying, senseless world. It's a modern protest song:

Oh, who did you meet, my blue-eyed son?
Who did you meet, my darling young one?
I met a young child beside a dead pony,
I met a white man who walked a black dog,
I met a young woman whose body was burning,
I met a young girl, she gave me a rainbow,
I met one man who was wounded in love,
I met another man who was wounded with hatred,
And it's a hard, it's a hard, it's a hard, it's a hard
It's a hard rain's a-gonna fall.

The forms and the poetic ideas are there to be used, where appropriate. What matters is that the voice and the concerns are yours.

Putting the two together: sonnets

A sonnet has a very clear internal and external shape. There are rules about the number of lines, and about the rhyme and the rhythm, and there are also rules about how the ideas should be organised. The rules are:

a) the poem is fourteen lines long

b) the lines rhyme alternately with each other in pairs:

When in disgrace with Fortune and men's eyes,
I all alone beweep my outcast state,
And trouble deaf heaven with my bootless* cries,
And look upon myself and curse my fate,

except for the last two lines which rhyme with each other:

For thy sweet love remembered such wealth brings,
That then I scorn to change my state with kings.

c) There are ten syllables in each line, with a stress on every second syllable:

When ín disgráce with Fórtune ánd men's éyes

If all that sounds rather complicated and unnecessary, the complete sonnet, by Shakespeare, might make things clearer:

When in disgrace with Fortune and men's eyes,
I all alone beweep my outcast state,
And trouble deaf heaven with my bootless cries,
And look upon myself and curse my fate.
Wishing me like to one more rich in hope,
Featured like him, like him with friends possessed,
Desiring this man's art, and that man's scope,
With what I most enjoy contented least.
Yet in these thoughts myself almost despising,
Haply I think on thee, and then my state,
Like to the lark at break of day arising
From sullen earth sings hymns at heaven's gate,
For thy sweet love remembered such wealth brings
That then I scorn to change my state with kings.

In this sonnet the speaker complains of loneliness (in the first four lines) and envy (in the next four lines). Then his thoughts turn to his loved one (in the next four) and he finally realises how lucky he is (in the final two lines). In this kind of sonnet, then**, the ideas are arranged in a particular pattern which is made clearer by the rhyme and also by the rules which govern how the lines are

* useless
** There are other kinds too: this one is known as the 'English' sonnet form.

arranged, the poem's structure. The first four lines go together, are 'held in' by the rhymes, as are the second four, and so on.

Here is a young writer putting those rules, and the principles behind them, into practice:

'The four men'

The man approached the place of the four men.
You come to take my sleep? said the sleeper,
I do not want your sleep, so sleep again.
You come to take my food? said the eater,
I do not want your food, I have enough.
Do you come for my thoughts? said the thinker,
I do not want your thoughts, your thoughts may bluff.
Do you come for my drink? said the drinker,
I have no thirst so drink all you can.
I am the joker and I come to fool,
I shall keep joking as when life began.
I'll take your heart and stuff it till it's full,
I'll take your brains and carve them with my knife,
And what I come for, I shall steal – your life.

Darrol Kenworthy

The author of this sonnet is eleven years old, but has an excellent instinctive grasp of what a poetic form is for. The lines form a pattern which *reflect* the pattern of the thoughts. The poem falls into two halves: in the first the men are uncertain as to who the visitor is, in the second he tells them. Within the first half there is also the question-answer pattern, which builds up suspense; and the most deadly words of the poem, 'your life', come neatly where they should, at the end, rhyming firmly with the line above to give a 'no argument' feel to it. His idea in the poem is that four men are visited by Death, but don't know who he is. He has used the poetic form to give shape to his thoughts, to help him *perform* his idea.

The section which follows outlines some forms and poetic ideas for you to try.

IDEAS FOR WRITING

Many of these ideas take the form of verbal games. Some will perhaps give you ideas for how to express what you already want to write about. Other ideas, e.g. haiku or writing a poem around a metaphor or simile are discussed in chapter 12 'Just a few lines' and in chapter 14 'New world, new forms'.

Ballads The traditional ballad form is often borrowed with successful results. Ballads tell a story, keep a regular length and rhyme pattern, generally four lines per verse. They include a large amount of dialogue, and often lead to a tragic end.

'Oh, where have you been, my long, long love
This long seven years and more?'
'Oh, I've come to seek my former vows
Ye granted me before.'

'Oh, do not speak of your former vows
For they will breed sad strife;
Oh, do not speak of your former vows
For I have become a wife.'

Their subject matter is frequently betrayal, by a lover or a comrade, but as can be seen in Dylan's song, the form can be adapted to new concerns, or tell stories in a modern context.

Refrain poems Another common feature of the ballad is the use of refrains – whole lines repeated at a regular point in each verse. These are common in folk songs:

There was a lady lived in York
All alone and a loney
A farmer's son he courted her
All down the greenwood sidey.

The second and fourth lines are the same in every verse. W.B. Yeats uses the enigmatic line 'Daybreak and a candle-end' as a refrain at the end of each eight-line verse in a poem about a wild old man determined to go on living notoriously. The poem on page 143 uses the line 'The rain fell hard, the mines, the dead' at the end of each verse. Used well, a refrain can reinforce the emotion of a poem with great effectiveness.

Telling a story There are of course lots of different ways to tell a story in a poem. These are just three.

a) Through a series of telegrams or postcards in which the reader has to 'read between the lines' to find out what is really going on. A young woman writes to her boyfriend, and we gradually guess that something is being concealed; an explorer sends cables home which become increasingly bizarre; a soldier abroad begins to change his mind about what he is doing there. You could adopt the form:

'His first postcard read . . .
His second postcard read . . .'

b) Through dialogue, as often in ballad forms. This is very good for creating suspense, when one of the speakers becomes increasingly anxious while the other remains calm.

c) Through monologue, where a character tells the story. It may become evident to the reader after a while that the character's view of things is not perhaps a sympathetic one.

Acrostics These provide a structure which at its simplest level is an entertaining verbal game, but which can also be an exercise in wit or satire. The letters of a word are spelt in capitals down the page. Each line of the poem has to begin with that letter and say something about the subject. This is by a Junior school child:

Catalogue –
As you know,
This has
Articles listed in it.
Looking for something?
Oh, then look in this book.
Good for you, there is everything here.
Uncertain? Trust us.
Everything O.K?

How about BUREAUCRACY or ADULTERY or POSSESSIVENESS?

Contrast poems Simple poems built on contrasts, using forms like (and of course these can be used ironically or in a bizarre way):

I used to be . . . but now I'm . . .
Yesterday is . . . tomorrow . . .
What I like about x is . . . what I hate about y is . . .

Echo poems A form used by George Herbert in the seventeenth century in which every other line consists merely of an echo of the last part of the previous one. The sound must be the same, but the spelling, and therefore the meaning, may be different. In Herbert's poem, the echo emerges as the voice of God:

O who will show me those delights on high?
Echo: I.
Thou, Echo, thou art mortal, all men know
Echo: No . . .
Then tell me, what is that supreme delight?
Echo: Light
Light to the mind: what shall the will enjoy?
Echo: Joy

Personification This means, simply, depicting something abstract, like love or spring or time, as a human being. A battle between two personified things – war/peace, love/jealousy, sleeping/waking, could provide you with the basic structure for a lively poem, particularly if you give them rather unconventional attributes.

14 New worlds, new forms

The twentieth century has seen an extraordinary amount of experimentation and seeking out of new forms in writing, as has happened with all the arts. As a teacher of creative writing I was frequently faced with students' demands for explanations of, and introductions to, concrete poetry, free verse, stream-of-consciousness fiction, absurd theatre, imagism, the 'new novel', 'found poetry', etc. It can all be quite confusing, and might either make you back away from anything which isn't familiar and traditional, or, equally bad, make you feel a has-been because you're working hard on trying to write a few 'straight' short stories. Although not all these questions can fruitfully be dealt with in one chapter, it should be interesting to have a look at a few of the ways that writers, and students of creative writing, have experimented with new forms of poetry and prose, as there is much enjoyment and stimulus to be got out of such activity and a lot of curiosity waiting to be satisfied.

I don't propose here to start speculating about why this has happened. It is put down to anything from the decline of religion to the invention of the camera, and there's truth in both those and anything in between. Of course, artistic forms have always been changing, but never quite so fast, nor so diversely, as in our century. Perhaps we can limit ourselves to isolating three broad, and of course interlinked, areas of change. First, the development of interest, prompted largely by the growth of depth-psychology, in the mysterious workings of the mind. This focused attention sometimes on the group but much more concentratedly on the individual, his motivations and the complexities of his moment-by-moment existence. While George Eliot's *Middlemarch*, published in 1871, deals with a whole community over a period of years, James Joyce's *Ulysses*, published in 1922, even more massive in length, covers one day in the life of two individuals.

Secondly, as traditional certainties about morality, religion, society, began to crumble, it was inevitable that traditional art forms, which for so long had expressed those certainties, should be challenged too. The whole value of art and its purpose in society was thrown into question. The twentieth century is the age of artistic 'movements', all of which had differing ideas about what art should be. Writers became more self-conscious, and freer in their attitudes towards language. Writers in the nineteenth century had been at pains to reflect the realistic feel of living, and novels in particular reflected this. Their successors in the twentieth century wondered whether there might not be a deeper level of reality which could best be reached by different means. Why should dialogue in a play sound like ordinary speech and the play itself reach a satisfactory conclusion? Why should the plot of a novel follow chronological sequence if important things could be explored by overturning it? Why should poems be locked in the same mould as those of the century before?

Finally, the enormous impact of modern technology upon society was bound to be reflected in the things people wrote. Literature borrowed from the cinema in particular in its techniques, and at the same time reflected an increasingly technology-dominated world.

All this is not only extremely superficial, but may also appear irrelevant to the general purpose of this book. It is likely, however, that readers coming for the first time to a page of James Joyce, for instance, or an e. e. cummings poem, are likely to be merely baffled or bored if they have no idea what to expect. The categories I've divided the material into are quite arbitrary, and there's bound to be some overlap with other chapters. But this is inevitable. The dividing line between 'orthodox' and 'unorthodox' is bound to be unclear.

Playing with shapes

The idea behind a 'shape poem' or 'concrete poetry' (the two are not necessarily the same) is not, as it happens, particularly new. In the early seventeenth century, the religious poet George Herbert wrote a poem called 'Easter Wings' in which the poem was printed on the page in the shape of a bird with outstretched wings. More recently, 'shape poems' have appeared in the form of wheels, stars, snakes, faces, and so on. This itself is quite fun, and children especially usually enjoy it. But after a couple you're tempted to ask what is gained in poetic terms by writing down your snake poem in the shape of a snake. Is the poem itself, its 'meaning', improved or even affected by the mould it's being squeezed into? Frequently not. But there are more things you can do by tinkering around with the conventional typography (the way a piece of writing is arranged on the paper) of a poem. This is by the Liverpool poet Roger McGough:

40 –	LOVE
middle	aged
couple	playing
ten	nis
when	the
game	ends
and	they
go	home
the	net
will	still
be	be
tween	them

Here the poem not only develops the fairly common idea of the ball game:

Ping	Pong
Ping	Pong
Ping	SMASH

– but develops it to make a wry comment on the relationship between the two players.

Still within the definition of a 'shape poem', here's one by a student of mine:

'The lover of the nile'

Beginning
at the
mouth,
he lingers,
between
the
Pyramids
then slowly
continues,
till,
passing

over
the
mount,
he
finds
himself
in
the
Valley
of the
Kings.
Basking
in the
warmth,
he
languorously
explores each
bank,
then
with
a
sudden
thrust
surges
up
the
Nile,
until
he ends
his
journey
spent,
in
the
interior,
where
it
all
began.

The typography lends much to the overall poem, not only following the winding of the river Nile, past the monuments on its banks, but also contributing to the poem's other more important feature, that of lazily and entertainingly describing love-making at the same time. The poem isn't only a visual joke, but one which exploits in a fairly elaborate way the potential of double meanings.

Both these poets, but particularly Roger McGough, rely on the overall 'shape' of the thing they're describing to give their poems impetus. We read the poem as a whole, because without the outline shape much of the effect would be lost. Words are used as bricks with which to build the whole. In the next poem, letters themselves, the bricks of the bricks, are separated out and reassembled in intriguing ways, which essentially is the difference between a shape poem and concrete poetry. This was written by the poet Edwin Morgan, for whom this kind of writing is a speciality:

'Message Clear'

 am   i
                         if
i am   he
    he r   o
    h   ur   t
   the re   and
    he   re   and
    he re
 a   n d
    th e r   e
i am   r   ife
              i n
       s   ion and
i   d   i e
 am   e res   ect
 am   e res   ection
              o   f
    the   life
              o   f
  m e   n
       sur e
    the   d   i e
i   s
       s e t   and
i am the sur   d

  a t res   t
                   o   life
i am he r   e
i a   ct
i   r u   n
i m   e e   t
i   t   i e
i   s   t and
i am th   o   th
i am   r   a
i am the   su   n
i am the   s   on
i am the e   rect on   e if
i am   re   n   t
i am   s   a   fe
i am   s e   n   t
i   he e   d
i   t e   s   t
i   re   a d
  a th re   a d
  a   s   t on   e
  a t re   a d
  a th r   on   e
i   resurrect
                      a   life
i am   i n   life
i am   resurrection
i am the resurrection and
i am
i am the resurrection and the life

Well, whatever's going on here the first impression is of somebody or something trying to make a statement, or more abstractly, of a statement trying to be made. Success is finally reached in the last line. I think it's a good poem because that is our initial impression and it's the most important one in the poem. Our effort, then, to understand is similar to the effort the voice' is making to be understood. You make it 'work' (it would be unfair to not to make this clear at some stage) by imagining the final sentence potentially printed in full on every line, with the poet only 'punching out' selected letters along the line, which when read straight across, make increasingly good sense:

am i
if
I am he
hero
hurt
there and
here and
there
I am rife
in
sion and
I die
a mere sect
a mere section
of
the life
of
men [and so on]

Finally the message becomes clear: 'I am the resurrection and the life', when the statement is read in its totality. It is as if a computer was pushing out punched cards all of which are partially right, but only completely right at the end. It could also be seen as a history of the developing power of Christ, beginning in confusion, through 'a mere sect', to 'I am the erect one, if I am rent I am safe. I am sent', to the triumph of the final statement.

Playing with words

That last poem was as much 'playing with words' as 'playing with shapes'. And there's a sense in which all creative writing is 'playing with words'. But I am here more concerned with a particular kind of word-play in which new words are invented, or old ones used in an unconventional way, or old words are put together to make new ones.

There is one famous instance of a style in which words are consciously always doing several things at a time, and that's James Joyce's *Finnegans Wake*, published in 1939. This large book seems to be one night's dream sequence of a Dublin tavern keeper as portrayed by the stream of his consciousness. Joyce creates hundreds of 'portmanteau' words, which take elements from different words and put them together to make a single word with several meanings, and uses puns and allusions everywhere.*

> Well, you know or don't you kennet or haven't I told you every telling has a taling and that's the he and the she of it. Look, look, the dusk is growing!
>
> O, my back, my back, my bach! I'd want to go to Aches-les-Pains. Pingpong! There's the Belle for Sexaloitez! And Concepta de Send-us-pray! Pang! Wring out the clothes! Wring in the dew!

Here the sounds of words are manipulated in an attempt to make them extend and enrich their meanings. But however intriguing such a passage is, the drawbacks of a sustained narrative in this style are obvious. It's such heavy going. It could be satisfying only if our linguistic resources, and our patience, came close to Joyce's. Unsurprisingly, the book is more read about than read.

Once you begin to invent new words and coin your own expressions you run the risk of either being downright unintelligible, or bogging your reader down in a linguistic swamp. Here's one instance, though, of a writer experimenting with the vocabulary of the language and being, I think, marvellously successful. It's taken from the beginning of Anthony Burgess's *A Clockwork Orange*, set some time in the not very distant future:

> 'What's it going to be then, eh?'
>
> There was me, that is Alex, and my three droogs, that is Pete, Georgie, and Dim, Dim being really dim, and we sat in the Korova Milkbar making up our rassoodocks what to do with the evening, a flip dark chill winter bastard though dry. The Korova Milkbar was a milk-plus mesto, and you may, O my brothers, have forgotten what these mestos were like, things changing so skorry these days and everybody very quick to forget, newspapers not being read much neither. Well, what

*Joyce's daughter Lisa was becoming schizophrenic at the time that he was writing the book. He took her to see the psychoanalyst Jung, convinced that his daughter's schizophrenic word games were no different from his own. 'You are both going to the bottom of the river' Jung told him 'but she is falling and you are diving.' There is certainly a similarity, though the tone is different, between Joyce's linguistic 'diving' and the way some schizophrenics describe their state of mind: 'I'm a no-un, an in-divide-you-all' (Quoted in R.D. Laing's *The Divided Self*)

> they sold there was milk plus something else. They had no licence for selling liquor, but there was no law yet against prodding some of the new veshches which they used to put into the old moloko, so you could peet it with vellocet or synthemesc or drencrom or one or two other veshches which would give you a nice quiet horrorshow fifteen minutes admiring Bog And All His Holy Angels And Saints in your left shoe with lights bursting all over your mozg. Or you could peet milk with knives in it, as we used to say, and this would sharpen you up and make you ready for a bit of dirty twenty-to-one, and that was what we were peeting this evening I'm starting off the story with.

Although the vocabulary is unfamiliar, it's not impossible to decode, and quickly becomes easy to follow, because it's consistent and because it already has some connections with ordinary talk. We pick up that 'veshches' means drugs, that 'droogs' are mates, then there are the Russian-based words, which are effective in giving a sense of a Britain very different in 'feel' from now – here we have 'moloko' for milk, and 'horrorshow', a sinister blend of English with the Russian word for good, later we find 'devotchkas' for girls, 'malchicks' for boys. There are also complete phrases like 'a bit of dirty twenty-to-one' with their air of casual cruelty. The mixture of violent, futuristic slang and recognisable English creates a sense of a world that is scary and brutal, and recognisably British. Alex's way of speaking becomes anything but a swamp. It takes the reader, on the contrary, straight into the heart of the experience at the most fundamental level, that of language.

Bombs, bureaucrats, bargain buys

As we have seen, Edwin Morgan's 'computer' poems suggest possibilities of drawing on the forms of modern technology in writing. It's interesting to note that (unlike 'Message Clear') most examples of such writing turn the language and form of modern technological society back against itself in satire. The treatment of the individual in mass society, for example, is a common theme. The student who wrote the 'Love Letter' opposite uses that inescapable modern phenomenon, the application form.

'Love letter'

PLEASE PRINT ALL ENTRIES

Name In full **Last** **First** **Middle**
Mr

Number **Street** **Road** **City/Town**

State **Code** **Previous address, if any**

Tel. no.

Marital Status Married/Single/Divorced/Widowed/Separated/**Explain**

Date of birth (Mnth Dy Yr) **Place of birth**

In case of emergency notify **Relationship**

Ever seen me before Yes/No/Don't know **Explain**

Names of my friends you know **Explain**

Height Weight **Wear glasses** Yes/No/Don't know

Handed Left/Right/Ambidextrous **Physical defects** Yes/No/Don't know

Explain

Education

School **Marks obtained at O or CSE level**

College **Marks obtained**

Habits

Reading Yes/No **Explain** Literature/Light Romantic/Historical/Psychological/Magazines/Pornography/Newspapers/Can't Read

Sports Yes/No **Explain** Cricket Football Hockey/Table Tennis Golf/Tennis/Never Selected

Films Yes/No/Explain (Art/Musicals/Formula/Suspense/Crime/Happy Endings)

(No. of films seen per month)

Skills

Number of girls been with **Explain**

Like taking them out Yes/No **(Dinner/Concert/Films)**

Hold hands while walking Yes/No/**Explain**

Kiss Yes/No **Explain** (Good-Night/Birthday/Otherwise)

How long do you expect the relationship to continue Few months/Less than that/Few Years/More than that/**Forever**

Do you like me/respect me find me Attractive/Worth being with/Beautiful

It is agreed and understood that false statements, if any, on this form may be considered sufficient ground for the termination of the relationship, as soon as discovered.

Signature/Thumb impression

Although there are one or two inconsistencies in the questions being asked (It's not entirely clear whether the person who is filling it in has ever met the person who is to receive it), the idea is a good one. It's entertaining, and salutary, to see in action something as impersonal as an application form trying to get its teeth round the delicacies of an emotional relationship. The very fact that it should take this task upon itself in the first place is of course the basis of the satire.

The emotionally stunted world of market research is again held up for scrutiny by the contemporary English poet Peter Porter, in a rather more elaborate and scathing way, again using a characteristic feature of modern society to make its point. The poem is called 'A Consumer's Report', and although the thoughts are continuous, they can also be seen as successive answers to a manufacturer's questionnaire:

'A Consumer's Report'

The name of the product I tested is Life,
I have completed the form you sent me
And understand that my answers are confidential.
I had it as a gift
I didn't feel much while using it,
In fact I think I'd have liked to be more excited.
It seemed gentle on the hands
but left an embarrassing deposit behind.
It was not economical
and I have used much more than I thought
(I suppose I have about half left
but it's difficult to tell) –
although the instructions are fairly large
there are so many of them
I don't know which to follow, especially
as they seem to contradict each other.
I'm not sure such a thing
should be put in the way of children –
It's difficult to think of a purpose
for it. One of my friends says
it's just to keep its maker in a job.
Also the price is much too high.
Things are piling up so fast,
after all, the world got by

for a thousand million years
without this, do we need it now?
(Incidentally, please ask your man
to stop calling me 'the respondent',
I don't like the sound of it)
There seems to be a lot of different labels,
sizes and colours should be uniform,
the shape is awkward, it's waterproof
but not heat resistant, it doesn't keep
yet it's very difficult to get rid of
whenever they make it cheaper they seem
to put less in – if you say you don't
want it, then it's delivered anyway.
I'd agree it's a popular product,
it's got into the language; people
even say they're on the side of it.
Personally I think it's overdone,
a small thing people are ready
to behave badly about. I think
we should take it for granted. If its
experts are called philosophers or market
researchers or historians, we shouldn't
care. We are the consumers and the last
law makers. So finally, I'd buy it.
But the question of a 'best buy'
I'd like to leave until I get
the competitive product you said you'd send.

There's not *only* humour in the way that everything the consumer says about life can be applied to any consumer product like soap powder – there's also a nasty feeling, stronger towards the end of the poem, that the consumer is so thoroughly brainwashed by advertising that he or she really does look at life as if it were no more than a commodity, ideally wipe-clean and hygienic, designed for eye-appeal and quick disposability. It's a satire on the whole consumer mentality.

That mentality is an essentially passive one, cowardly even, in its refusal to face up to ugliness and suffering, and the twentieth century is remarkable for having developed an ability to obscure unpleasant or inhuman facts with abstract or cosy language. This is the language of propaganda, whether of the advertiser or the politician. The public relations element is deep in all of us now. We call a new way of doing maths in schools SMILE (Schools Mathematics Individualised Learning Experiment), we call genocide 'pacification', and forced marches 'relocation of personnel'. It can be comic, or sinister. Writers haven't been slow to respond to this, notably George Orwell whose essay 'Politics and the English Language' is full of excellent advice about writing in general. One student of mine came up with this original idea, an extract from a manual on 'Civil Defence'.

'Civil Defence Manual'

In the event of enemy action
Preparation is of vital importance.
This manual has been prepared
With just such a contingency in mind.

In case you have been hit from behind
(while enjoying the sunset etc.)
We will use the key word 'SMILE'
S – Stop bleeding by applying direct pressure or cold compress.
M – Maintain body temperature by wrapping yourself in a blanket (if possible, induce a vacuum)
I – Imbibe emetics in case of poison in the system (not in case of acids)
L – Lure away danger by positive means (avoid being unscrupulous)
E – Either use sling or splints to guard against further damage.

In case of bites from Aves, Pisces, Reptilia,
Amphibia, Mammalia including Homosapiens
the following treatment is prescribed –
Wash and dab wound with antiseptic
(In case of insane mammalia/Homosapiens
ignore completely so that wound bleeds freely)
If bitten by reptilia
the size, age and sex should be determined
before applying tourniquet and incising wound
to remove all trace of venom.
For all the above cases the important
Pass word is 'Do not Panic'

The above emergency methods are not required
if following precautions are taken.
A built-in warning system should be installed.
At the least sign of 'possible enemy' approach
the alarm should be tuned to blast
Assemble at Static Mobile Post.
On receipt of instruction from Control room
or messenger, action must be taken.
The safety of crowds should be sought.
Do not turn your back on the enemy
Also do not face the enemy
Without protective, warm clothing.
Conversation if not totally absent
should be kept to the barest minimum
Do not leave any part exposed,
to protect against possible bites
If frightened, smile, say 'Good morning/afternoon/evening'
(It will help to avoid physical contact)
and be off.

This chapter has necessarily been a rag-bag of different unorthodox ways of writing. Nor is it implied that anything which appears in other chapters is necessarily to be described as 'orthodox'. The word 'experimental' has been stretched to cover many things. There is a difference, for example, between the one-off attempt to do a particular thing ('Love letter', *A Clockwork Orange*) and the development of an entire prose style suitable for the full range of experience. Joyce spent seventeen years on *Finnegans Wake*, and said of it 'I felt I could not use words in their ordinary connections . . . When morning comes of course everything will be clear again . . . I'll give them back their English language . . .' 'Morning', however, didn't come, and Joyce's style can be counted experimental in our terms in that the book is now ignored except by scholars. The passages in this chapter have been chosen to give the reader some idea of the possibilities and, occasionally, dangers, of unorthodox writing. My general belief is that there is a lot of enjoyment to be had from taking chances with styles and forms for a specific purpose. The development of a particular personal, strongly unorthodox *style* however, is filled with dangers of imitation, obscurity and pretentiousness, dangers which only a few writers manage to overcome to make their style really work for them. What the reader finds appealing or stimulating here will have to be, as usual, a matter of personal choice.

IDEAS FOR WRITING

A noise poem: describe an experience or an activity solely in terms of the noises made during it, by people or things (e.g. riding a horse, a thunderstorm breaking, a man trying to start a car).

Break the conventions of everyday language and try a piece of experimental prose describing a particular violent or ecstatic experience. Do anything you like with punctuation, spelling, layout, etc.

A twentieth century manual on murder, carefully written in a language that smoothes over the nature of the facts being discussed. Or, in the same vein, a twentieth century marriage contract.

The government probably has a taped radio announcement ready to play to calm the population in the event of a nuclear war. Write your version of that radio announcement.

Two modern lovers go through a 48-hour crisis in their relationship by sending a rapid series of telegrams to each other. Write those telegrams.

Pages from a diary of the future. Sketch some details of everyday life in the twenty-first century, remembering that the language will have gone through some changes by then.

Computer-designed love letters and christmas cards. Alternatively, write a series of letters between a human being trying to redress some fault, and the computer who deals with his letters.

A series of glossy, consumer magazine advertisements, which exploit the methods and language of modern techniques of persuasion, for tanks, nerve gas, nuclear shelters . . . or even an abstract thing like love, or religion.

Take a historic sentence and use it as the basis for a concrete poem. Experiment with the typography and layout for different effects (see 'Message Clear' on pp. 157–158). For example:

Poets are the unacknowledged legislators of the world
Laugh and the world laughs with you
Let him who is without sin cast the first stone.

15 *A bit of drama*

Setting up situations

A sixteen year old school kid surprises a male and a female teacher kissing in a stockroom in which he has left his motorcycle. The ill-feeling that arises leads to him holding a lighted cigarette over the petrol tank and keeping them, and himself, prisoners . . .

(*Gotcha* by Barrie Keefe)

A man in a New York park falls into conversation with another man on a bench. He tells him at length about the difficulties he has with a ferocious dog who inhabits the stairs up to his flat, and the complex measures he takes to defeat, or win round, the dog . . .

(*Zoo Story* by Edward Albee)

Two identically dressed men with despatch cases meet on an empty stage and exchange crazily jumbled clichés of patriotism and diplomacy. They sign pieces of paper, then tear bits off them, becoming increasingly angry, then manic, as they dance around the stage like schoolboys, making noises of gunfire . . .

(*Out of the Flying Pan* by David Campton)

Some young people are at a party. Suddenly the lights fuse, and they are left in darkness. (How this works on stage is described later). The power does not return for some time. Needless to say, they don't sit in silence waiting.

(*Black Comedy* by Peter Shaffer)

A man and a woman sit facing each other. She is worried by something, he takes a rather patronising interest. But what is it she is worried by?

she: I can't help it.
he: Can't help what?
she: Getting into this.

he: Getting into what?
she: If I could say I wouldn't be in it.
he: What's it like?
she: It's terrible.
he: In what way?
she: I can't say. That's why it's so terrible . . .

(Adapted from *Do You Love Me?* by R.D. Laing)

The curtain goes up and the audience is confronted with another audience opposite them watching a stage, on which the body of a man lies sprawled over the settee. A man in the audience noisily rustles his programme, another eats a box of chocolates – theatre critics. They begin to chat . . .

(*The Real Inspector Hound* by Tom Stoppard)

All of these situations have provided the basis for good pieces of modern drama. The shortest, the dialogue which begins 'I can't help it', lasts about seven minutes; the longest, Peter Shaffer's *Black Comedy*, lasts around an hour. While *Out of the Flying Pan* is circular, ending as it begins, *The Real Inspector Hound* is a bizarre, complicated whodunnit involving the theatre critics themselves. None of these is a conventional, realistic, two-hour, three act, half-a-dozen characters kind of play. Whatever each of the playwrights chooses to 'do' with the subject matter, the situations themselves provide an immediate interest, whether through an instantly felt tension or a curiosity at the unusual spectacle on the stage.

In a conventional full-length play, it is generally character (what the figures on the stage are like as people), and plot (the story in which they all play a part) which provide the main interest for the audience. This is not wholly true of the plays described above however, and need not be true at all. This chapter, in fact, isn't about writing *plays*, if by a play we mean something that realistically tells a story in about two hours, which is in itself a very limited definition. Besides, it's very difficult to keep an audience interested in watching half a dozen people talk to, or even murder, each other for a couple of hours. It might be more useful to describe a play as a 'piece of drama over (say) five minutes long, needing one or more people to act it, in front of one or more spectators'.

When children play, they do not feel the need to convince their audience (if any) that a stick with a bit of green cloth on it really *is* a dragon, or a ring of chairs really *is* a fortress, or that a six year old really is the commander of the U.S. Cavalry. They simply accept the conventions of the game, of the play, and see what can be done with them – and that usually means, a lot. A lot not so much in terms of plot, but of performance, the fun, the excitement, the danger, that can be got out of setting up a situation.

'Setting up situations of dramatic interest' is what the playwrights whose plays are described at the beginning of the chapter have done, rather than thinking only in terms of a realistic plot with realistic characters told over two hours. This point is made not merely to encourage the inexperienced or time-starved writer to attempt some drama, but also because it is a feature of modern theatre, which has turned significantly away from realistic, full-length psychological drama towards experimentation. Since the early sixties, workshop theatres, travelling drama groups who play in pubs and community halls, street theatre groups, schools and colleges as well as TV and radio drama, have shown what can be done on a small scale, with a low budget, and using techniques which constantly open out our understanding of the conventions of theatre. (And as drama is above all a visual, active experience, it goes without saying that to see or hear as much as possible of this kind of drama, if only on television and radio, is essential.)

The conventions of drama

What are those conventions? The most familiar is that often known as the 'fourth wall', in which the audience looks in on, say, a sitting room, faces three of its walls on the set, and itself comprises the fourth one. The actors maintain the illusion that they are unobserved by anybody. It would be inconceivable, therefore, for any member of the cast to address the audience – this would break the spell. Nor would they speak aloud to themselves, as people do not generally do that in real life, or certainly not at any length; and the illusion of real life is essential in this kind of drama.

But of course this has not always been so in the theatre. In Shakespeare, for instance, characters very much do speak aloud to themselves (Macbeth, for example, expressing the terror in his mind before the murder of Duncan), or make asides to the audience, or introduce the play before it starts. In Medieval plays, audiences might be asked to pass judgement on the actions of a character, or listen while the moral of the story was pointed out to them. This technique, of recognising the existence of the audience, is now a fairly common part of modern drama. In John Osborne's *Luther*, the audience becomes the congregation when Luther preaches; in Trevor Griffith's *Comedians* the audience becomes at one point the clientele of a pub, before whom a group of trainee stand-up comics are put through their paces; in the plays of Bertolt Brecht, there are frequently figures who comment aloud on the action to the audience; in *Night and Day* by Tom Stoppard, one of the characters occasionally reveals her thoughts to the audience, but the other characters are unable to hear her. The effect of breaking the 'fourth wall' convention in this way can be entertaining, involving, and some playwrights would argue, more faithful to the truth of the situation: what is being presented, after all, is a play and not real life.

Another convention which we often take for granted is that the audience knows from the beginning who the characters are, and where they are. But uncertainty can be fruitful: it is important that the man and woman in R.D. Laing's 'I can't help it' are nameless, generalised, non-realistic, that they are typical of all of us and the knots we tie ourselves into. In David Storey's *Home*, we listen to the conversation of the two main characters for some time before we become aware that the setting is a mental home. Had we been aware of this from the start, we would undoubtedly have been tempted to distance ourselves from the characters, to categorise them as mentally ill and therefore different. This device also ironically undermines the question of 'what is real', of obvious relevance in a play about a mental home. At the beginning of the short play *The Lover*, by Harold Pinter, a wife and her husband discuss the wife's lover. In the next scene, the husband is out and the lover enters. The lover is played by the same actor who has played the husband. With the same people playing the wife/mistress and the husband/lover, the business of role playing naturally comes under scrutiny as the play progresses. They are after all the same people, only in different roles.

The breaking of the conventions of realism in this way creates numerous possibilities, and is especially suited to brief, experimental drama. While the next two devices are taken from longer plays, both are theatrical 'tricks' which would work well in a shorter piece. In the previously mentioned *Black Comedy*, the stage opens in darkness but we hear the sound of drinks being poured and the chatter of party conversation; the record player then dribbles to a halt to signify a power cut, so the lights come up and the characters begin to grope around as if they were in complete darkness. The trick is wholly convincing, and delightful to watch. There is a similar reversal, this time with language, in Brian Friel's *Translations*, in which the Irish characters are portrayed speaking only Irish, though they in fact speak English on stage, and the English only English. The audience is thus able to understand what both sides are saying, while the characters understand only what is spoken in their own tongue. There is even a love scene between a young Englishman and an Irish girl, in which neither of them can understand a word the other speaks, and yet manage to communicate and express their own rapture in an extraordinarily moving way. While this is a device, it is not merely a gimmick: one of the main concerns of the play is the way that language unites and divides human beings.

Situations which are of immediate dramatic interest, however, are not created only by tinkering with theatrical convention, or by abandoning realism. Any situation of tension or conflict which needs no painstaking build-up (the discovery of somebody doing wrong, a husband and wife waiting outside a divorce court) will serve as potential material for a short play. The theatrical potential of explosive situations is exploited by the many playwrights who use theatre for political purposes. They are less concerned with depicting the complexities of personal relationships, or playing games with theatre itself, than with a bold presentation of aspects of conflicts and contradictions in society. Barrie Keefe, for example, in the short play mentioned earlier, *Gotcha*, uses the boy holding the cigarette over the petrol tank to express responses to modern education which are not intended to be seen as the moanings of one particular rejected individual, but as a condemnation of society's values.

In a slightly longer play, *Mama Dragon*, Farrukh Dhondy analyses different attitudes to black unrest, from those of liberal white social worker, and fake-radical black girl who sleeps with him, through bottle-throwing aimless young blacks, to organised guerilla violence. The setting is a community club in Brixton around the time of a proposed National Front march. The dramatic tension is created by the arrival of an older black youth who has finished his stint with the army in Northern Ireland, where he has learnt the techniques of street warfare, and stolen a deadly flame thrower, a 'mama dragon'. The dramatic question 'will he use it?' is linked to the moral and political one of his justification for doing so.

Both *Gotcha* and *Mama Dragon*, then, quickly set up situations which are dramatically and politically explosive. In both plays the audience forms a 'fourth wall'. Both plays are straightforwardly realistic. Dhondy's play, however, also features songs by a reggae group at the edge of the stage, which are woven into the narrative. In the same way, much theatre which unashamedly sets out to preach a message uses music, dance, mime and so on, as if to announce 'We're not going to pretend that we're not trying to teach you something, so we might as well make it as entertaining and interesting a lesson as possible'. Joan Littlewood's *Oh, What a Lovely War*, a satire on the First World War, strings together songs from the trenches and music halls, speeches of Earl Haig's, casualty statistics, sketches of international tycoons shooting wildfowl and discussing the profits of the arms trade, and so on. The audience is presented with continuous novelty and ingenuity, a variety-show freshness, but the humour is often dark, the message bitter.

What kind of dialogue?

So far in this chapter the emphasis has been on ways of thinking about drama generally, other than in terms of straightforward realistic plays. This is not the place to touch upon the vast area of mime, or improvisation, or working with sound and light effects, all of which can help to make a dramatic experience. But there remains, for the writer at least, whatever the techniques chosen to achieve the results desired, the central question of dialogue. While this is certainly crucial, it has been left till last because writing dialogue cannot be discussed in isolation from the question of the 'style' of the piece of drama. Put simply, the considerations of writing realistic dialogue are not necessarily the same as those of writing dialogue for a more experimental piece. What follows, then, are examples and discussion of dialogue written in different styles, written in progressively less realistic modes. As ever, there are no iron rules about writing dialogue, but a few useful points may arise in the course of discussion.

The scene is an interview room in a police station on general election night. Karn, a detective, has been listening to results on the telephone, looking forward to the Thatcherite 'new dawn'. He is waiting to see a black suspect, Delroy, whose wife has been found bleeding to death in their flat while Delroy was in the pub.

Delroy has not mentioned his wife's death, and we learn later that he is quite unaware that anything has happened to her. Wilby, the detective constable, has told Karn that Delroy believes he is there on 'sus', on 'suspicion'.

He replaces receiver. WILBY enters with DELROY. Pause.

Delroy: We ain't been introduced. My name is Leon Delroy.

Karn: How very civilised Mr Delroy. How very nice to make your acquaintance. D.C. Wilby and me, D.S. Karn.

Delroy: Well, well – this is a nice room. I haven't been in this room before.

Karn: Décor's quite simple. Let me show you around. We've gone in for the hardwearing but easy to clean.

Delroy: Do you get a lot of mess in here then?

Karn: You never can tell.

Delroy: Very nice. Very, um, simple.

Karn: Same with the furniture. I trust you approve?

Delroy: Well I . . . What did you say your name was?

Karn: Karn. K A R N.

Delroy: Is that German or something?

Karn: It's my father's name. His father gave it to him and he gave it to me. Sort of family heirloom.

Delroy: Nice.

Karn: Handed down from generation to generation. All English. Pure stock.

Delroy: Well, this looks the most comfortable chair.

Karn: Then sit down, do sit down Mister Delroy. Take the weight off your feet. How long did you say you were in the boozer?

Delroy: From about sevenish.

Karn: More than three hours solid boozing! Then my gawd-fathers, you must be fucking worn out Mister Delroy. I do apologise. Perhaps, Wilby, you could bring in a chaise-longue to make Mister Delroy here a bit more comfortable.

Delroy: You're too kind, Mister Karn, but this'll do. As it happens, I haven't got too much time to spare tonight. I'm in a bit of a hurry. We're going down to the club to watch the election results.

Karn: The club, eh? What one's that? Beefsteak? Brooks? White's or the M.C.C.?

Delroy (laughing): I ain't fussy.

Karn: That's nice to hear.
Delroy: As it happens, Working Men's Club. But if you was thinking of inviting me to one of them –

(from *Sus*, by Barrie Keefe)

The audience is being asked to believe that these are three real people in a real situation. Accordingly the characters say nothing that a hard white policeman and a young black man might not say in real life. Good realistic dialogue, like this, has to capture the audience's interest, convey information, reveal characters, develop a situation, all at the same time. To do this, Barrie Keefe creates an atmosphere of light-hearted combat between the two men, played out at the level of wit . . . at least in Delroy's case it is light-hearted. Karn's has a sour, menacing edge to it:

Delroy: Well, well – this is a nice room. I haven't been in this room before.
Karn: Décor's quite simple. Let me show you around. We've gone in for the hard-wearing but easy to clean.
Delroy: Do you get a lot of mess in here then?
Karn: You never can tell.

The apparent good humour of Karn's remarks about his name being passed down as a 'sort of family heirloom' is belied when he continues with a hint of menace to his black suspect, 'Handed down from generation to generation. All English. Pure stock'. A dramatically tense moment. Delroy chooses to ignore the remark. The audience cannot. If there is any one rule of dialogue it is that of economy: nothing that anybody says should be superfluous or repetitive, but should serve to move the play forward, whether in terms of action, ideas, character, information, tension.

One of the reasons why this dialogue is interesting to listen to is that both characters have a natural wit, an instinctive way of fencing with words, particularly in a sarcastic way. Anybody writing realistic dialogue, however, has to come up against the fact that many people are inarticulate and do not find words coming readily and interestingly to them. You can end up writing dialogue which reflects this, and which is thereby wholly 'true-to-life', but which could have the audience shifting impatiently in their seats and wholly losing interest in characters who are coming across simply as boring people with nothing to say to each other. As with any kind of dialogue, in prose fiction too, it is never enough simply to let two 'ordinary' people talk to each other and call it realism. Not all realistic dialogues (like those in real life, for instance) are interesting to listen to. Frequently a compromise is reached in stage dialogue: the majority of characters in such plays are in fact rather more articulate than people are in reality, if not in terms of unlikely vocabulary, then in terms of wit, or the imagery of their speech, or its rhythms: a measure of 'unrealism' acceptable in return for lively dialogue.

An odd *feel* of realism, in dialogue that is in fact quite extraordinary, can be found in the next exchange, between an old tramp, Jenkins, who has been surprised by Mick going through Mick's brother's things in their dingy flat.

Mick: What's your name?
Davies: I don't know you. I don't know who you are.
Pause.
Mick: Eh?
Davies: Jenkins.
Mick: Jenkins?
Davies: Yes.
Mick: Jen . . . kins.
Pause.
You sleep here last night?
Davies: Yes.
Mick: Sleep well?
Davies: Yes.
Mick: I'm awfully glad. It's awfully nice to meet you.
Pause.
What did you say your name was?
Davies: Jenkins.
Mick: I beg your pardon?
Davies: Jenkins!
Pause
Mick: Jen . . . kins.
A drip sounds in the bucket DAVIES looks up.

You remind me of my uncle's brother. He was always on the move, that man. Never without his passport. Had an eye for the girls. Very much your build. Bit of an athlete. Long-jump specialist. He had a habit of demonstrating different run-ups in the drawing-room round about Christmas time. Had a penchant for nuts. That's what it was. Nothing else but a penchant. Couldn't eat enough of them. Peanuts, walnuts, brazil nuts, monkey nuts, wouldn't touch a piece of fruit cake. Had a marvellous stop-watch. Picked it up in Hong Kong. The day after they chucked him out of the Salvation Army. Used to go in number four for Beckenham Reserves. That was before he got his Gold Medal. Had a funny habit of carrying his fiddle on his back. Like a papoose. I think there was a bit of the Red Indian in him. To be honest, I've never made out how he came to be my uncle's brother. I've often thought that maybe it was the other way round. I mean that my uncle was his brother and he was my uncle. But I never called him uncle. As a matter of fact I called him Sid. My mother called him Sid too. It was a funny business. Your spitting image he was. Married a Chinaman and went to Jamaica.

Pause.

I hope you slept well last night.

(from *The Caretaker* by Harold Pinter)

Again, there's little here that, in theory at least, an ordinary man like Mick couldn't say, no grand phrases, no long words, no poetry. In fact though, and the effect is dramatically very powerful, Mick's way of speaking is bizarre and frightening. It's bizarre because he chooses to tell the extraordinary story of his 'uncle's brother' at such a time, and frightening because his motive for doing so, in this utterly confident delivery, must remain unknown to Davies and the audience. It gives a weird sense of total, and ruthless, control. There is even something studiedly cruel about the way he tosses in words like 'penchant' and 'papoose', words which would be quite unfamiliar to Davies. On top of all this, it's also darkly funny: the details of the story itself make no sense at all ('I think there was a lot of Red Indian in him . . . Married a Chinaman and went to Jamaica'), and Mick's self-congratulatory way with words ('Nothing else but a penchant') is comic in the way that all show-offs are comic. But he's also a bully, and Davies isn't laughing. Characters in Pinter's plays, and this is a feature of much modern drama, use words to conceal what they mean just as much as to reveal it. And while on the *surface* the dialogue in the extract from *Sus* does not greatly differ from the dialogue here, the characters in the play do at least say what they mean.

The final extract begins to move resolutely away from realism, away from the pretence that what the audience is watching is real, towards the feel of an 'act' being presented to the audience. This is taken from a brief satirical sketch on modern statesmanship, performed at an Aldermaston rally. The feel of the 'double-act' is strengthened by the intentional absurdity of much of the dialogue. Two men, A and B, meet on stage. They carry briefcases. The sound of departing aircraft suggests a remote airfield. They shake hands.

> *B [orating]:* This is a hysterical evasion. I come daring the olive. Branch. Our signatures on the Charter will ensure that between our two hate stations will be established a bite of peas, to be enjoyed by our childrens, and our childrens and our childrens – and our childrens. My country devours nothing but peas, will never devour anything but peas, has never devoured anything but peas. Success crown our forts. Piece of Fiendship.
> *[He steps back to the sound of applause. He indicates to A that the floor is his. A steps forward, and clears his throat]*
> A speaks, spouting the same kind of nonsense. Then:
> B: Over?
> A: Done.
> B: Business?
> A: Business.
> *[A and B each bring a chair into the centre of the stage and sit facing each other]*
> A: Chairman?
> B: Chairman.
> *[A stands up]*
> A: Open.
> *[He smiles at B, and sits again. They smile at each other, and take sheafs of documents from their despatch-cases. Frowning, they hand documents to each other]*
> Section A, paragraph B.
> B: Sentence Y, Segment C.
> A: Portion U.
> B: Caution D.
> A: One for you.
> B: Another for me.
> A: Afterthought I.
> B: Compromise E.
> A: Page in Code.
> B: Here's the key.
> A: Postscript W.

B: Exhibit G.
A: A two-hour session, and we break for tea.
B: Clause P.
A: Memo three.
B: Division two.
A: Revision V.
B: B.
A: C.
B: D.
A: E.
B: G.
A: P.
B: Tea.
A: I.T.V.
B: B.B.C.

[Each now has the other's pile of papers. They stuff them into their despatch-cases again]

A: Yes?
B: Yes.
A: Then nothing remains to disturb our complete agree ment, and without further ado I shall produce the Treaty.
B: Since nothing remains to disrobe our complete greed-ment, without further ago you may produce the treat. He.
A: The Charter.
B: The Barter.
A: The Carter.
B: The Garter.
A: Legato.
B: Regatta.

[A produces an ornate document with seals dangling]

B: Check?
A: Check.

(from *Out of the Flying Pan* by David Campton)

The distortion of the language of diplomacy ('Our country devours nothing but peas' etc.) is designed to emphasise its emptiness, as if they can say what they like because it doesn't mean anything and nobody's taking any notice anyway. The treaty signing is broken off with predictable moral indignation and insults, and world war ensues. Not particularly difficult to write, but an effective idea, and good to watch.

Obviously, most of the appeal lies in the tricks with language: it would be impossible to maintain this over a longer period. The non-realistic nature of the dialogue in Samuel Beckett's full-length modern classic *Waiting for Godot* makes it a hard play for some people to enjoy from start to finish. But, to repeat the point made at the opening of the chapter, there are many possibilities open to anyone who wishes to try their hand at drama which falls outside the limitations of the full-length play. All that is needed is a few ideas, and the energy to try them out. Some suggestions follow on the next page.

IDEAS FOR WRITING

These are 'situations for drama' rather than 'plots for plays'.

A group of ventriloquists and their dummies (played by real people) sit in a waiting room before auditions with an agent. The ventriloquists talk to each other about their acts. The dummies are also able to talk to each other, 'unheard' by the ventriloquists, whom they discuss with some liveliness.

A youth club. An ex-member arrives, on the run from the police (it could be uncertain as to whether they are innocent or guilty). There is disagreement among the members as to whether they should shelter the fugitive, and what part if any the youth worker(s) should take.

A child is visited by the ghost of one of his (or her) idols – a figure from history, a dead sports star, a comic book hero. The ghost accompanies him through various scenes, with his family, girl-friend, at school, making comments, offering lighthearted advice, talking to and listening to the child. Their conversation, of course, can be heard by the audience, but not by the other characters.

In Tom Stoppard's play *After Magritte*, the curtain opens on a stage which looks like a scene from a modern painting: a man stands wearing green rubber fishing waders and little else, a lamp-shade hangs on a pulley balanced by a fruit filled basket, and an old woman lies on an ironing-board, furniture is jammed up against the door. The play then proceeds entertainingly to account for all this, and ends with another bizarre 'picture'. This is an idea that can be fruitfully adapted, with quite different situations. It's the drama equivalent of setting out to write a short story which will include (say): a plastic Buddha, a derailed train, two sets of identical twins, an unsigned postcard from Brazil, and a consignment of polo mallets. The fun for the writer is to link them together in a coolly far-fetched way, the fun for the audience or reader to watch that being done.

A teacher and an ex-pupil meet after some years in an unexpected situation: the pupil could be a policeman apprehending a suspect, a burglar caught red-handed, a prostitute amazed (and amused) at the identity of her client, a tax-inspector interviewing an alleged tax evader. As long as the situation is somehow difficult for at least one of them, perhaps comically so, there is material for a short play.

A group of people find themselves unable to leave a space, say a dentist's waiting room, or the dining room at a dinner party, or the large lift of a department store, or the place in which they are being held hostage by a gunman who speaks little English. The reason could be mysterious – have they in fact been gathered for some purpose? Is this their last judgement? Or it could be practical – the lift has broken down and cannot be mended for some while. How will this group of perfect strangers react, and how will they pass the time? This could be anything from realistic comedy to thriller to surreal farce.

An interviewee for a job is directed to the wrong room. The interview begins. The interviewer and the interviewee become progressively more interested or puzzled by each other's view on the 'job' as the misunderstanding persists.

After the funeral of a wealthy relative, the family gathers to hear the reading of the will. Various snippets of conversation could be spotlit (hypocritical, complacent, sentimental – keep it light) while the other characters 'freeze' and are less brightly lit. Then the will is read: it contains several surprises, in its tone, in the comments the author makes about their relatives, in what it reveals about the dead person's past life, in the way they have decided to distribute their wealth. A surprise 'mystery character' appearing at the end would provide a nice dramatic climax.

Use the idea of Peter Shaffer's *Black Comedy* (itself borrowed from classical Chinese theatre: such ideas are there to be borrowed) in which all the characters 'lose' their sense of sight in a blackout. All your characters – a family at dinner, or guests at a party, or even a single pair of lovers, temporarily lose their sense of hearing. They themselves can only communicate with gestures and hand signals, but their thoughts are spoken aloud to themselves, and therefore to the audience.

A play for radio, or your own tape recorder. The advantage of this form is that you can use sounds and voices to suggest feelings, and movement of time and place. (Dylan Thomas' famous play for voices *Under Milk Wood* deals with the dreams and fantasies of a sleeping Welsh village, for instance.) An old woman sits dozing in her armchair. In her head she hears the voices of people from her past life. Or a group of children who have never met have the mysterious ability of mentally communicating with each other across the country, or across continents. They are obviously excited about their gift, but also frightened by it. What will they do with it?

A reading list

In addition to the reading list of short story writers on pp.122–23, here is a very brief (and personal) summary of some things it might be useful, and enjoyable, to read.

Nineteenth-century classics

George Eliot's *Middlemarch* – a study of a small provincial community – is in many ways the definitive nineteenth-century realist novel, with its broad sweep of characters, its keen social observation, and strong moral concerns – as well as a terrific plot.

Even more gripping is Wilkie Collins' *The Woman in White*, a Victorian mystery story that is also wonderfully well written.

Of Dicken's novels, perhaps *Bleak House* best combines Dickens' extraordinary imagination, satirical edge and compassion (not to say sentimentality): slightly weirder but equally compelling are *Little Dorrit* and *Our Mutual Friend.*

All the Jane Austen novels, but particularly *Pride and Prejudice* and *Emma* are marvellous displays of the English ironic style, subtle but devastating.

For the best example of nineteenth-century Gothic, *Wuthering Heights* by Emily Brontë is a powerful tale of love and obsession in appropriate wild moorland setting.

If you're curious about the great Russian novels, then two very different examples can be recommended: Tolstoy's *Anna Karenina* is a rich and minutely observed story of an adulterous relationship struggling to survive in a hostile society – a 'social' novel; while Dostoevski's *The Brothers Karamazov* is a huge, extraordinary tale of three brothers (a thinker, a lover, a saint) and their quest for fulfilment a 'philosophical' novel.

Twentieth century

For a taste of pre-war British fiction and its concerns (e.g. men vs. women, the struggle for spiritual values in an ugly and oppressive modern world do try: *Howard's End* by E. M. Forster, *To The Lighthouse* by Virginia Woolf and D. H. Lawrence's semi-autobiographical *Sons and Lovers*.

Continental fiction has tended to be more interested in ideas than British fiction, particularly ideas of existential alienation, the sense of the individual's absurd position in an incomprehensible world: Kafka's *Metamorphosis* and *The Trial* are classics of this kind, as is Albert Camus' *The Outsider.*

American fiction is a vast area and I'm making only a few suggestions. The idea of the dream – whether political, personal or spiritual – and its failure is a common one in American writing, and can be found in, for example, Herman Melville's huge masterpiece about a man's pursuit of the great white whale, *Moby Dick*; but also in the elegant but fearful emptiness of Scott Fitzgerald's high society fable, *The Great Gatsby*.

The classic novel of modern teenage angst, its pain and disillusion, is J. D. Salinger's *The Catcher in the Rye*; while Vladimir Nabokov's *Lolita* offers a more middle-aged but equally passionate, and dazzlingly written, journey through fifties America.

John Updike's 'Rabbit' tetralogy – *Rabbit, Run, Rabbit Redux, Rabbit is Rich* and *Rabbit at Rest* – is a marvellous portrait of an American individual's progress through the post-war decades. A different sort of social history can be found in Toni Morrison's Beloved, a heartbreaking (but brilliantly inventive) account of the trauma of slavery. For a sense of modern consumerist America – its television shows and shopping malls, its restless vacancy – there can be no better novel than Don DeLillo's extraordinary *White Noise*.

Two classics of modern world fiction are Gabriel Garcia Marquez's *One Hundred Years of Solitude*, an enchanted history of a South American village, and a novel that owes much to Marquez, *Midnight's Children* by Salman Rushdie, which weaves the story of modern India into the tale of a boy with magical powers born on the stroke of midnight on the first day of Independence.

Two books can claim successfully to have illuminated the 1980's, the so-called 'decade of greed': Martin Amis' Money, a hysterically funny portrait of a grotesque media hustler, addicted to pornography and fast food; and Tom Wolfe's *The Bonfire of the*

Vanities, an ambitious satirical account (more high class journalism than literature) of what happens when Manhattan high society meets the ghettos of the Bronx.

Experimental writing

There are a few pieces of 'experimental' fiction that really work, that cannot be described simply as experiments. For example, the stories of Italo Calvino, particularly his *Invisible Cities*, portraits of cities of the mind, sustained by an idea or an emotion. Russell Hoban's remarkable novel *Riddley Walker* is a triumphantly inventive glimpse of a Britain centuries after a nuclear holocaust, clinging to and reinterpreting the scraps of history that have survived. Like *Riddley Walker*, Anthony Burgess's *A Clockwork Orange* is written in a bizarre language heavily adapted to give a sense of a future society familiar but also frighteningly different to our own.

The fictions of Argentinian Jorge Luis Borges, particularly the collection *Labyrinths*, are brilliant speculations on intriguing philosophical ideas. What would life be like, for example, if a man were able to remember the tiniest detail of his life and experience? Or enter an infinite library? Or achieve longed-for immortality?

Poetry

Even harder to choose from, but four poets of this century can be said to be essential. The Irishman W. B. Yeats' poems ('Sailing to Byzantium', 'Under Ben Bulben') are extraordinary explorations of the power of myth in a post-Christian world. Equally driven by a spiritual quest, but not so much of a showman, T. S. Eliot charted a course from despair (*The Waste Land*) to religious hope (*Four Quartets*).

Since the war, two poets stand out: the first, Philip Larkin, ironic, self-reflective, comical about sex and gloomy about death, and author of two of the most currently quoted ironic snatches of verse:

'They fuck you up, your mum and dad'

and

'Sexual intercourse began
In nineteen sixty three';

the second, Ted Hughes, who evokes the ferocity of an amoral natural world in powerful, muscular imagery. Many, however, prefer the stunning confessional poetry of his estranged wife, Sylvia Plath, poetry which probes the wounds of the psyche with a pitiless imagination.

Drama

There are a handful of twentieth century plays that demand to be seen or read. Samuel Beckett's *Waiting for Godot* is the touchstone of modern Absurd drama, wittily dissecting the futile journey of the modern soul; Harold Pinter's *The Caretaker*, full of menace, dark comedy and wonderfully bizarre dialogue occupies an almost equally eminent place, and is, it has to be said, an easier read than *Godot*.

Look Back in Anger by John Osborne became known as the first (and best) play by the so-called Angry Young Men of post-war Britain. There's plenty of anger in it, certainly, at the complacency and hypocrisy of British society. Not all of it has worn very well, but there are some terrific set-piece tirades.

The plays of Arthur Miller tower above all others in the world of naturalistic theatre, theatre that reflects the feel and concerns of contemporary society (as opposed to the more philosophical theatre of, say, Beckett). Miller's *Death of a Salesman* is an attempt at a modern tragedy, the story of a man who goes under when no longer able to match the pressure to succeed – emotionally as well as professionally – in competitive America.

Of playwrights writing now, perhaps the most interesting are: David Hare (*Murmuring Judges*), David Mamet (*Glengarry Glen Ross*), Tom Stoppard (*Jumpers*), Trevor Griffiths (*Comedians*) and John Guare (*Six Degrees of Separation*).

Index

LIBRARY, UNIVERSITY OF CHESTER

Printed in the United Kingdom
by Lightning Source UK Ltd.
130385UK00001B/297/A

9 780713 648508